Following early experiences of union with the infinite, Conor Patterson explored the spirit realm. At the age of twenty-four, he received an astonishing initiation on a beach when thousands of figures appeared and descended into him. He subsequently searched for answers through teachings and techniques before the spontaneous and unaided recognition of his nature became clear. With this he began a simple life of authentic expression, and the space from which this text flows opened up.

IS

Spiritual Wisdom for a Chaotic Age

CONOR PATTERSON

Watkins Publishing
London

This edition published in the UK in 2002 by
Watkins Publishing, 20 Bloomsbury Street, London, WC1B 3QA

Cover design by Echelon Design
Cover photograph © PhotoDisk
Designed and typeset by WestKey Ltd
Printed and bound in Great Britain by NFF Production

British Library Cataloguing in Publication data available

Library of Congress Cataloging in Publication data available

ISBN 1 84293 053 2

www.watkinspublishing.com

Acknowledgements

My primary gratitude is for existence. To be alive is amazing and wondrous. Let us honour this in celebration.

I would like to thank all beautiful and interesting beings connected to *Is* along the way including Leanne Jones and Siobhan O'Donnell for giving me some concrete feedback, Mervyn Wright and Siobhan Patterson for their early interest, Julie Evans for her companionship on many of my adventures, Alan Jacobs for his friendship and agency, Michael Mann for his publishing, Mira, Ramesh Balsekar, Jagadish Parikh and Swami Chandresh for their teaching, Amy Downey for her house-sharing, Renate Wendl-Berry for her facilitation of my growth, Jamie Buxton for his printing, Aine Lynch and Duncan Campbell for their participation in Spirit People, and to all my siblings and friends for their love and intimacy. May the growing continue!

About the book

In *Is*, Conor Patterson reveals that the unity we seek is inherently *who we are*. To recognize this is to begin to honour our nature. When and how we recognize this is uncontrollable and utterly spontaneous.

However, there is a major threat to this recognition - the moral code that we learn as we grow up. Morals give an inappropriate importance to mental judgement, and the overwhelming effort to apply them can leave us feeling tired and forgetful.

This book describes what happens when morals spontaneously collapse and the struggle to do 'right' ends. It shows that when we focus less on our mind's chatter and more on our heart's song, then we can finally unleash our potential by dancing to that song in an honorary celebration. Shedding the light of the heart over all practical aspects of life, *Is* explores morals, struggle, purpose, searching, death, belief, acceptance, desiring, control, power, emotions, relationships, mind, body, love and unity.

Is describes:

- The reasons we struggle in our lives and what happens when those struggles cease.

- The difference between living a limited life based on moral values and living an unlimited life based on your heart's values.
- What happens to you on a personal level when love and unity spontaneously take over your life.
- What we are as spirit.

These writings are not instructional, nor are they prescriptive. They are not doctrine and they are not something to practise. They have no motivation, intention or hopes. They are essentially meaningless. Although I am editing and holding the pen, these words are simply appearing. This is not a mysterious 'channelling'. This is an absorbed expression of 'isness'. These writings are isness expressing itself through my conditioned perceptions and language. They flow in enjoyment and love.

Words are simply a style of expression. They mean nothing in and of themselves. They are the flavour of what they point to. To speak of the whole is solely poetic. There is nothing to say about that which has no differences. Words describe the fragmentary world of things. Applying them to a description of isness is our only way to chat about isness. I use written language for the sake of communication. As such, the text is not a serious exposition of existence. We only gain this through our own recognition.

The extrapolation of someone else's experience is of little use. Reading, listening or discussing the 'correct' or 'best' way to be in life is a futile attempt, and one that involves struggle. No teaching, knowledge or acquired information will ultimately reveal isness. Isness is *what is*. Any pointer to isness is actually part of isness. Pointers in the form of teachings, observations, lectures, books and talking are absolutely useless in terms of *honouring* isness. To honour what is, is to *let it be who you are*. No formula can teach us how to be who we are, because we are *already being it*.

If you read these writings, forget them and listen to your own. Any practical application of them may result in struggle.

So, enjoy as you please, and take none of it too seriously. You are welcome to write to me at the publisher's address about any aspect of this book, or to share your own views and experiences. You can find further information on my website www.conorpatterson.com

Thank you for sharing this amazing phenomenon we call life.

Conor Patterson
Hove, East Sussex,
England
February 2002

If you must seek,
seek not for enlightenment,
but for entitlement.

Sustained peace comes not from running from the world or making changes within the world. Sustained peace is our inherent nature and it can only be clouded by ignorance and denial. To recognize our inherent nature is to give up looking for peace in the world and to rejoice in the peace that we *are*.

Contents

CONTENTS

CONTENTS

1 *A Story*

When I was a child I had a strong feeling that, as I grew older, a great secret would be revealed to me. I was excited and curious. When the time came for revelation, I was amazed to find that the 'secret' was nothing new. It was simply a clear recognition of my unlimited nature.

I am 'isness'. Isness can be described as 'all that is'. There is nothing outside of it. When there is a clear recognition that we inherently *are* isness, along with an honour of that, then the struggle to be 'something we are not' ceases. This is a revolution in contentment, and the key to everlasting peace. My own journey into the realms of recognition and honour was an exciting adventure full of fear, doubt, passion and awe. I experienced extremes of isolation, despair, unity and peace.

In the late 1980s, during my teenage years, I craved recognition of my innate unity. I felt that something was missing and that somehow I did not belong to the pursuits that had been placed before me. By the age of sixteen, I had dedicated my life to rediscovering the unity that I am. I could not rest contented until I once again became aware of my nature. In my mid-twenties, the clarity that 'I am isness' returned and the recognition I yearned for was back again, this time with the added boon of consciousness. When the recognition and honour of my inherent nature became stable, I celebrated and am continuing to do so today. The stories in this chapter give a flavour of the events surrounding this growth.

Absorption

On a sunny day in March 1997, I wandered on the shore of a volcanic lake in Guatemala. As the sun sank towards its resting-place, I stopped on a rock, and knelt there. I had been magnetically drawn to that lake and to that rock yet I had no idea of what was about to follow. The blue waters lapped by my side and I felt a sense of wonder and anticipation. Then it happened. I fell into complete absorption…

I am everything
Everything is I
In our total sameness there is nothing
This is the supreme unity
This is my oldest friend.

This is so amazing
I can't contain the awe and excitement.
I am dead
I must be.
The villagers will find my corpse here with a huge smile on its face
Everything has gone and so have I
There is only white light.

I have no body.
    I can hear only one thing.
        There is only one sound in the whole universe.
        Water.
    The glug of water against rock.
    I am on a rock.

I can see. I can see differences now. I can see the water lapping at the rock. The universe is crystallising around me. Water, rock, sky, sun, clouds, birds, insects, people. Love. Overcome with a sense of wonderment and a feeling of gratitude that knows all hearts to be one.

This experience of complete absorption brought with it the simple yet absolute recognition of my inherent unity. Since then, I cannot dispute that clear recognition that 'we are all one'. Everything that has ever existed and ever will exist simultaneously exists in unison. It is the experience of that indisputable unity that can propel anyone into an awareness of his or her nature. The human race seems intent on believing that we are somehow isolated from the incredible unity of the life. Our 'spirit' is seen as a small part of us that exists 'somewhere over there'. Success is commonly measured on how great and powerful the fragments of one's life can become. When this happens, unity is sought by attempting to enlarge the parts of one's life, rather than stepping back from them to see them as a whole. The new car, the better job, and the improved relationship can do wonders for our personality but it will not earn us unity. We *are* unity. My absorption experiences healed me from a sense of isolation and showed me that the infinity of the universe resides within every single one of us.

The experience of absorption is such a deep immersion in the whole that the ability to construct or perceive boundaries is temporarily lost. My earliest experiences of this, like all humans, were in babyhood. These became periodic as I grew older and almost totally petered out in teenage years. In my late teens, as I grew out of a conditioned denial of my inherent nature, experiences of absorption become more common for me. After each experience, the recognition of my inherent unity flickered on and off. I tried to convince myself that if I continued to recognize my inherent unity, then I might surpass the need for recognition. I was scared and excited by this prospect for I believed that this was the key to my contentment. My dear values of power, status, control and purpose were threatened. I tried to deny my unity in the hope that I could somehow suppress it. I used every strategy that I could grasp, but to no avail. My life was struck with abundant beauty and gradually the struggle to stay limited ceased.

Along the way, the recognition of my nature became more and more stable. Every influence I came across in some way added or subtracted from this stability, although I can give no credit to any single influence. Absorption experiences were central to my growth into appreciation of isness. They encouraged the confidence in me to be boldly honest about the nature of existence. During my day-to-day fragmented experiences, they stood as a platform from which I could see oneness. I quickly fell in love with the spontaneous experience of unity, and was continually grateful for the miracle of it.

Through such absorption, I became able to taste the full flavour of isness.

It can be said that absorption is a move from the fragmentary world of many things into the realm of absolute unity. Such a shift is what makes an absorption experience, yet at the moment of absolute unity there is no experience for there are no longer any boundaries to separate an experiencer from what might be experienced. There is also no 'unity' or 'wholeness', as there is no longer anything to be united or made whole. The experience drifts in later as boundaries reform. Our psyche brings back a fairytale of a land once visited, a land that cannot be experienced when actually in it.

The experience of having been in absorption ends, just like all experiences. However, if that experience is spontaneously committed to as being a genuinely profound happening and not merely a trick of the material world, then the recognition of 'all existing as one' can continue even after the experience has gone. With this recognition the boundaries of life can be treated as a game. In my life, continued recognition gave way to the awareness of the essential unity that I am. This awareness affords me the comfort of play. I can rest contented in the unity of a fragmentary world.

Direction

One cool August night in 1998, I sat by the shore of the English Channel. The beach around me glowed with the last dying embers of a fire. The sky was awash with stars and as I looked up at them, I experienced a spontaneous stillness. All of a sudden, a white flash of light burst in the sky, expanding into a large circle above me. A few seconds later another one came. Each time, I experienced them as a benevolent explosion in my heart. Then, to my amazement, I saw swarms of figures descending from the sky. They seemed to be classic mystics of the past. I could recognize people like Osho, Jesus and Buddha. There were thousands of them. They circled around me, turning and spinning, and then they somehow deposited themselves inside of me and settled there.

The sky became still again. I fell into a deep reverie, and rocked in the beauty and awe of what had happened. Minutes later, a name came to me. *Makay Cono Bub.* It seemed to come from above me. It has been suggested to me that this name came from the astral plane. If it came from a British Airways plane, it would have made no difference to what I experienced.

I would describe this remarkable happening as a spontaneous initiation. I was enlivened, enriched and dumbfounded. The next morning, elated and grinning stupendously, I was feeling a little perturbed. I felt the need for some guidance, so I closed my eyes and asked for a sign to show me what I was to do. I opened my eyes to see a plastic shopping bag that read, 'Lighten the Load'. Since that day, lightening the load has been happening in my life and often in the lives of those around me.

Influence

My most influential teachers have been from my immediate environment. Water, in particular, has been a consistent source of revelation. The strength, stillness, consistency and ease of water are a joy to behold. Being around it invokes those same simple qualities in myself. Sitting by rivers, lakes and the sea, I have witnessed the authenticity of water, and its wonderful inability to dishonour isness. It is what it is, and it makes no effort to be otherwise. It simply flows. It flows around any obstacle in an apparent display of acceptance. Water irresistibly attracts me to become that same simple flow and to move in the elegance of acceptance.

The diverse simplicity of environments like forests, beaches, jungles, mountains, lakes and rivers has stirred within me a deep reverence for the simplicity of my own nature. It is like an alignment. To be immersed in the vast wonders of infinite beauty is to invigorate the recognition that the very same beauty lies within one's self. Such environments have no ability to be other than what they are.

The sheer authenticity of nature contrasts sharply with the intellectualized and compartmentalized structures of the human race. In a city, or a house, the shapes that meet the eye are products of the mind. Straight lines, machines, advertising and the like are all engineering feats invented in the human mind. In the countryside, the shapes are beyond the domain of the mind. A fern, a tree or a snowflake can be identified, copied or mutated by the mind, but not produced by it. Although we may attempt an understanding of nature, the complete isness of it is incomprehensible. To a mind that has been strengthened by an exaggerated belief in its own abilities, the beauty of organic environments can restore a sense of balance.

Seeking

By the age of twenty-five, I had experienced many passing episodes of deep contentment and was convinced that this was something that extended beyond mere fleeting experiences. I believed it was something that could last forever. I set out in search of everlasting contentment and in doing so, the struggle of discontentment intensified. To be discontented and to assume that there is nothing else is definitely less of a struggle than to be discontented and know that contentment is possible!

I searched as if I was to discover a magical elixir of immortality. I looked all over. Even as I fell into contentment, I continued looking. When I became increasingly aware of my inherent unity, I kept on looking. I meditated, I prayed, I sought masters, I read the words of wise ones, I walked, I ate, I danced, I created, I practised, and I tried. Along the way, I enjoyed the search, and I enjoyed the struggle. Sometimes I think I must have enjoyed it too much for when the time came to give it up, I was rather reluctant. I see now that enjoyment is an essential ingredient in the appreciation of existence. All our lives are stories and it matters not what the story tells if we are enjoying it.

The irony of my searching was that by looking for my own essential nature, I was denying it. We are who we are. When we look for who we are, we are ignoring that. The search to reach awareness, enlightenment, contentment or realisation is the last attempt at dishonouring one's nature.

When we move into honour of our unified nature, we can intuit the cost of it. Our life values of control, personal power, and purpose along with the cherished stress of struggle are either lost or changed beyond all recognition. The search for contentment is the last chance to deny our nature before we spontaneously flower into honour.

No one can give to us that which we already are. What other humans can do, though, is influence us in ways that add to or take away from our appreciation and understanding of isness. As humans, we are fragments of isness. As beings, we are the whole of isness. Another human can influence the way we perceive ourselves and the way we express, describe and appreciate isness. However, no person or thing can influence that *we are isness*.

Opening

In 1999, on a quest for everlasting peace, I found myself on top of a mountain in Nepal. Okay, it is a typical strategy, but that is all I had up my sleeve at the time. I meditated, practised yoga and studied ancient scripture. I lived with yogis and Buddhist lamas. The thread of their teaching was renunciation. Throw away unnecessary burdens and watch what happens. The ensuing simplicity leaves a space within which the beauty of authenticity can flow. I studied with Swami Chandresh, a yogi who had meditated in solitude for twenty years. It was fun to be with him and I formed some beautiful friendships.

On one occasion, I walked up a Himalayan mountain. As I ascended, I became increasingly light-headed and enjoyed sustained laughing fits. In combination with my sense of surrender, these changes in oxygen levels created a very pleasurable experience. It was on my arrival at a Hindu pilgrimage site that I met a man claiming to be the Olympic Champion of Laughing. He had obviously been training well and had a magnificent effect on those around him with his huge head-thrown-back laughs.

When I left Nepal, I visited the jungles of India. Upon arrival, I climbed straight into a mango tree and experienced a dissolution of boundaries, then a complete immersion in isness. Luckily, on this occasion, I did not fall out of the tree. I spent my time in these jungles in a bemused ecstasy where every leaf was a 'yes' and every deer's cry was a prayer.

Upon my return to England it was as if my home, possessions, business and identity belonged to someone else. Everything appeared differently. My life had taken a huge shift and I could not neatly slot back into my previous role. So, rather than struggle, I gave away or destroyed most of my possessions, finished up my electronic multimedia business, and left home with one bag. Stopping only for a solar eclipse in Devon, I made my way to Clare on the west coast of Ireland. I was drawn there by the continuing quest to find peace everlasting. I craved contentment and knew it existed. I gave my life to the discovery of it.

Focus

Renunciation is not essential to focus on the inner world. However, if one has a history of concentration upon the world of objects and experience, then renouncing this outward-facing focus can provide a vacuum that may be filled by an inner focus. Redressing the balance means focusing on the direction that has been neglected in the past. To get stuck in looking either inwards or outwards is to deny that we live in both.

By exploring the realm that lies beyond experience, I found a balance that healed the disparity between inner- and outer-looking. Living in Clare, I experienced a growing contentment. I was focused on *tantra*, *ayurveda*, meditation, *yoga*, scripture study and living a simple life by the sea. I continued my search by spending time with teachers including Mira Pagal, Ramesh Balsekar and John de Ruiter. Some of them claimed to have reached a special state, while others were authentically passing on information or simply being themselves.

It was a fascinating time, travelling around and seeing what these people had to say. I was a little confused as I felt that I had already reached the end of my search. Although this made the search absurdly unnecessary, I yearned so much for the grail of everlasting peace that I tried anything. After asking many questions in many countries, I gave up in despair. I was trying hard to aspire to reaching a state that I believed others had attained. Somehow, I had got caught up in a 'race for enlightenment'.

Part of my growth during this time was to become aware that just because someone is sure of himself does not mean that they are necessarily 'right' or 'truthful'. I could see that no teacher could provide the guidance that I was seeking. A few teachers became dear friends, while I resented others for pushing their denial onto me. I found that where teachers had an interest in hierarchies, their wisdom was patchy. Such teachings serve to further the divide between spirit and form. Strictly imposing the wisdom of others upon yourself only intensifies struggle. I discovered this as my attempts to reach peace reinforced the morals that I had learnt as a youngster. I was inundated with 'wrongs' and 'rights', judging my actions and behaviour as 'good' or 'bad'. I used the moral codes of teachers, both living and dead, as my reference point for these judgements. It was of course impossible for me to live like someone else. Singing my own song was all I could do, and the attempt to do otherwise was an effort fraught with struggle.

I clearly saw how ridiculous the search was, and how much denial goes with it. The effort to search for enlightenment is a denial of your inherent nature. It is to search the whole world for the treasure that is sitting on your kitchen table. After a last intense effort to reach what I am, I gave up in failure. As I did so, I opened up to the recognition of my nature. I saw that the treasure had been sitting in front of me all along.

I had reached the end of the path but was afraid to admit it. My life work of finding eternal contentment would be over if I let it be that way. I had given up searching for any special state. I had learnt to listen to the silence of the heart and to follow it. I experienced a certain confidence to be who I was without question and without doubt. It was a simple honouring of 'that who I am', without needing to understand it or contemplate it.

During this time, all reference to a moral value system ceased. I was simply being. Thereafter, if morals were referenced, it was an intellectual exercise, and rarely channelled the flow of my behaviour. With no moral reference, who I am as isness can be appreciated with gratitude, and who I am as a human can uniquely express itself without attempting to be a clone.

The recognition that my heart, isness and I are one whole entity sustains an underlying contentment that shadows every mental, emotional and physical experience. In this recognition, I no longer needed to search for, or question, my own essential nature, for there it was in front of me, always present, as it always had been. In honour of it, I open up to the flow in every cell of my body, every thought of my mind, and every movement of feeling. I am the contentment that I once sought. As I honour that contentment, I appreciate more and more the magnificence of isness.

Inspired by others who had shared their talents, and unable to keep words away from paper, I gave myself in service to Is. It was a beautiful, spontaneous process. The text spilled onto paper, with the 'I' temporarily absent. The more a person popped up to take control, the more that flow was distorted. I got out of my own way, so to speak. Words appeared on paper and I stored them away until a dark winter when I collated them into the book you are now holding.

2 *The Moral Code*

Morals are the rules that we learn to base our decisions on. As we grow up our community teaches us the concepts 'right', 'wrong', 'good' and 'bad' both directly and through inference. The patchwork of morals that we are expected to adhere to is a code, a set of guidelines to live by. The moral code is used as a reference for behavioural rules. Morals tell us how to be, how to behave, and how to live. Following these 'how-to' rules while ignoring what your heart tells you restricts your capacity to honour your nature. When the moral code spontaneously dissolves, you can once again be released into the wilds of uninhibited expression. Our heart naturally expresses itself through the mind, body and emotions. Our heart is unlimited. If we place limitations on the heart's expression by using any control methods then we attempt to limit that which is infinite. If we live by any rules or codes, our capacity to allow direct and unrestricted expression is diminished. This dampens our experience of existence.

Roots of the moral code

The moral code is the structure that instructs new beings in the world. It tells them how to behave, what choices to make, where to go, and what to do. It is a set of invented signposts that shows us 'what to do and how to do it'.

The moral code was written for us long before our bodies left the womb. For generations before the birth of our body, our ancestors passed on the code, developing it as they did so. The moral code that we inherit from our ancestors is the structure that polices our character traits and attempts to conserve them. This is meant to ensure that we do not change too much, and that our character traits will be handed down to the generations succeeding us. This process of conservation keeps a human tribe bonded together by convention, tradition and moral discipline. To this end, every individual is inescapably born with a moral code embedded in him or her as a reference tool for behavioural discipline.

The irony of the moral code is that it originally began as an attempt to outdo isness. Most of our ancestors were not content with isness. They tried to better isness by getting something more. They also wanted to avoid pain. They created moral codes in an effort to gain control over their own lives and behaviour, with the subconscious hope that then the entire universe could be controlled. They hoped to become rulers of isness, but their perception of isness was tainted by dishonour. They yearned to break away from isness and to become separate from it. This, they hoped, would allow them to gain control over isness. However, separation from isness is impossible. We cannot control whether we are part of isness or not. The attempt to become separate from isness simply leaves us feeling isolated and frustrated. The moral code encourages the effort to channel life into a restricted and therefore 'controllable' form. This *always fails*. We do, however, naturally inherit this futile battle from our ancestors and this inheritance takes the form of the moral code.

Childhood morals

Parents project their moral code onto their children, usually subconsciously, in an attempt to guide them and shape them in their own moral image. A child that is limited by its parents' moral code inherits the frustration and struggle of constantly falling short of successfully adhering to it. The parent can reinforce limitations on the child through inappropriate punishment and reward. Where the child fails to comply, the parent projects their moral code in the form of punishment. Where the child succeeds in compliance, there is reward. In this way, the child is imprinted with its parents' 'limitations'. The parents' subconscious use of a moral code in an attempt to limit a child stems from a simultaneous wish for the child to succeed where the parent had failed *and* the hope that they will not. Any succession by the child leaves the parent feeling redundant. The 'best' the parent can make of this is pride. This pride is the claim that the child succeeded where the parent failed *only* because of the parent's influence.

A child without the imposition of a parent's moral code can grow into *any* form in *any* way without the guilt brought about from moral restriction. They can be who they are without struggle.

Obviously, a responsive parent caters for the physical, emotional and mental survival of the child, yet this does not have to involve morals. Morals are intellectual. The boundaries that a parent sets for a child's survival can come from the heart's response to instinct and biology. For example, preventing a child from stepping into a busy road can be the heart's response toward the biological urge to protect. Application of an intellectual moral is of little use to a responsive heart. A heart can only respond cleanly if it does not obsessively refer to a moral code.

The structure of the moral code includes notions of 'right' and 'wrong'. The building of the moral code progresses throughout childhood and is reinforced by the 'should'. 'Should' is used as a pressure-tool to ensure that children conform. Stepping outside of the 'should' often results in punishment. When this happens, a child learns that retribution is at hand when certain imaginary boundaries are crossed. This fear reaction keeps the child from crossing the boundaries too often. Moral limitations are thereby established.

The punishment given to children for stepping over the 'should' barrier often stems from a fear in parents that the child will destroy the moral code. The punishment then represents a protest by the parents against the demolition of moral codes. They are in effect reacting from the fear of their own moral code dissolving. A child displaying its inability to recognize the moral code imposed on it is a major threat to that moral code. This is because a complete ignorance of the moral code gives the code no opportunity to become more sophisticated. A code without obedience to its rules will perish. The parent must therefore attempt to enforce his or her own code on the child to protect that very code from being lost. If the child continually disregards the imposition of their parent's code, then the parent becomes scared of the consequences. They recognize that behaviour *can* exist outside of their moral structure and that the one behaving in such a way can do so without distress. The moral security that they have known becomes threatened. They react in fear by punishing the child, which in turn injects them with the same reaction. The child has then been infected by the boundaries of its parent's moral code.

So begins the struggle. Seemingly trapped within an imposed moral code, the child can sense its inherent freedom. There is a frustration because it knows its own nature, yet fears the punishment that will result if that nature is honoured above and beyond the moral code.

A new being in the world is gifted with teachers. At first, these teachers are not consciously chosen. They are the teachers of the community that surround a baby as it goes through childhood. They include parents, siblings, teachers and religious figures. The structure of the moral code is given to a new child as a synthesis of the many moral codes belonging to these teachers.

Teachers reinforce the establishment of the code by making certain choices attractive through reward, while others remain unattractive through punishment. The teachers who surround a new human therefore helplessly engineer the establishment of the moral code. They too were once new humans infected with the codes of their ancestors.

A human growing up in the current value system of power hierarchies will automatically adopt the ancestral moral code, neglecting the unity of isness in doing so. The inherited strategies of self-indulgence, ignorance and greed are attempts to survive in a world where humans are trying to claim supremacy over their fellows and over nature itself.

As babies, we can begin to know our nature. We are born with open hearts, and can be who we are without deviation. This authenticity is usually lost as we grow into competitive, thinking humans, too scared to be who we are. The values of control, power, and purpose are bound by a moral code and then worshipped, and our authenticity is subsequently lost. This leads to isolation, a feeling of disconnection from nature, and ultimately to the despairing contradiction of being who we are whilst trying with momentous effort to be something else.

The group chant

The moral code serves only one useful purpose. It gives us entry into the 'group chant'. The group chant is the song that is sung en masse by the community. It is the song that shows the popular consensus on the purpose of human existence. It is the way that everyone agrees to act in the world. It is the song that unifies everyone's behaviour. The moral code acts as a binding agent in the community as everyone understands the 'right' and 'wrong' way to behave and respects the implications of that. In this way, the community can learn the 'moral lyrics' of the group chant and sing it together to nurture a sense of belonging.

Variations of the group chant are sung all over the world. The group chant gives the new human the basic language for singing their 'own song'. To sing one's own song is to directly express one's inherent nature without pollution from the reward and punishment systems of the community's moral agenda. The irony is that although singing along with the group chant teaches us language skills, it also simultaneously limits the possibility of actually singing one's own song. The pressure to conform to the group direction stifles individuality in a way that usually deters any unique singing. The group insists we learn the chant, join in with it, and do not stray into our own variations, let alone create our own new song from scratch. Without chanters, the group chant would be lost, so the existing chanters do not want anyone straying for then they would be without a chant.

Policing the code

The guidelines instructed by the moral code insist on conformity. The fear of retribution and the consequences of moving beyond the code's boundaries act to keep a human guided within limitations. A powerful reaction to doing 'wrong' is also taught to the recipient of the moral code. That reaction is guilt.

Guilt is the taught reaction to moving past the boundaries of the code. Shame and dishonour is cast upon the one straying from the group chant, and the self-punishment of guilt is taught as an easy and effective way to keep them from dropping out of the chant. Guilt is the ultimate self-policing strategy. If everyone feels guilty about their own uniqueness, then no one need keep a watch on straying chanters. Anyone straying from the chant will punish himself or herself through guilt, and in this way the teaching of guilt is a most effective, efficient method of keeping the chanters conforming.

Guilt is essentially an emotional dwelling upon the 'wrongness' of doing 'wrong'. The new human is taught that the self-punishment of guilt is a useful structure to internally remind them of the limitations of the code. Guilt is the price to be paid for overstepping these restrictions. It is a 'safe' way to deal with your own deviation from the moral code by punishing yourself internally before an external force can do it for you. After so much punishment from others, the internal reaction of guilt can seem less harmful than external retributions, and so it is readily learnt. Breaking the moral rules results in punishment and if one can punish oneself early enough, then external punishment may be avoided. Even if external punishment results, guilt still provides an acceptance, acknowledgement and justification of the punishment. If the self-punishment of guilt is already in progress, then any external punishment will be harmonic with it. Such is the safety of the guilt reaction.

After childhood, the individual applies the policing of the code onto himself or herself more or less unaided. The situation produces a fascinating array of individuals each condemning their own 'wrong' actions and being proud of their 'right' ones. Meanwhile, except in extreme cases, the 'wrongness' or 'rightness' of these actions goes unnoticed by anyone else. There is rarely any reward or punishment system existing outside of a grown individual, so it is up to them to deter 'wrong' actions and promote 'right' actions for themselves. Judgement of one's own behaviour acts as a commonplace and necessary enforcement of the moral code. With little assistance from outside, the struggling individual must judge himself or herself heavily in order to maintain the moral structure. For this reason someone who is almost outside of others' moral enforcement, and who appears to be free from parents, religion or dogma, can often have the toughest moral regime going on inside. This balances the lack of moral guidance from the outside.

Breaching the code

You will continually and unintentionally breach any moral code simply by being who you are. Prescribed ways of being come from the 'controlled' realm of perception, a place where humans endeavour to engineer plots to overthrow isness and become supreme rulers over it. Being who you are, on the other hand, is totally uncontrollable. As such, moral codes cannot be honoured by simply being.

No one ever managed to match a moral code perfectly with his or her behaviour. Any natural impulse that contradicts the code must be repressed in order to stay within the code's confines. This can only be achieved for so long, before the repressed impulse rushes forth in a magnified version of itself. The form of such a release is often astounding and unpredictable. It is often surprising to the one who was repressing the impulse, as well as to those witnessing the amplified unleashing of it.

The irony of the moral code is that although the fear of retribution and the guilt reaction insist that the code be adhered to, *being* in the code cannot be controlled. The code can be broken simply by being in an authentic way. Inherent in every moral code is the inevitable consequence of breaking the rules.

The attempt to adhere to the code, to do the 'right' thing can have hilarious consequences in its failings. When we witness others' failings to live by their moral codes, it often has a humorous element no matter how grave it may seem. The nervousness of admitting that a moral code simply cannot contain one's behaviour is often accompanied by laughter. This humorous fun disarms the moral code by revealing its contradictions, often in areas of taboo like bodily secretions, sex, death and violence. Such comedy reveals the gap between the moral code and the behaviour of the one trying to live within it.

The unintentional breaching of the code can also be emotionally traumatic, of which a problem can be made. It is then that the repeated offence of the code's precepts gives one the opportunity to invent problems. After all, it is a problem for others – they want to maintain moral codes in an effort to retain their sense of purpose in the group chant. It is easy, therefore, to invent a problem for oneself from the struggle of breaching the code. The purpose of life then becomes to overcome this problem. It becomes a challenge to live in the 'right' or 'correct' way. However, this is deemed to fail from the outset, because the infinite nature of being means that any prescribed way of being will eventually always be contradicted.

Changing the code

Once the moral code is established, it is subject to change. Certain morals die and new ones are born. The influences on the code change. New friends, teachers and experiences all bear down on the code and modify it by their association. When the fluid ever-changing nature of the code is observed then the ability to change one's own code can be learned. This may appear as an escape route – a chance to broaden the moral code, to make its berth wider and allow what was previously forbidden to become acceptable. People commonly take this route in their teenage years. The perception may be held that at last there is a chance to go beyond the inherited moral code and live life in a 'freedom' from limitation. The attempt to reach 'freedom' can take the form of stretching one's own moral code. This brings the taboo 'wrongs' of the old inherited code within the accepted 'rights' of the new code.

Of course, the new 'rights' that are created only create further 'wrongs'. Such is the law of duality: one cannot exist without its opposite. The successful pursuance of more 'rights' within the moral code automatically produces the same amount of 'wrongs' to counterbalance it. Therefore each moral code is *exactly as limited* as the previous one. The moral codes of two different individuals always have the same amount of limitation. Where that limitation expresses itself can vary, but the restraint is the same: for as many 'right' ways there are to behave, there exists an equal number of 'wrong' ways. No code actually has a higher 'right to wrong' ratio than any other.

Every moral code appears to be an inescapable prison. Even the attempt to escape requires the belief that it is 'right', 'good', or 'best' to escape, and can therefore only revise the moral code.

3 Disintegration of the Code

While there is no escape from the structure of a moral code, one remarkable thing can happen: the destruction of the moral code itself. If the control mechanism of the moral code spontaneously disintegrates, then life can open up into a dance of unlimited expression. When we cease to hold on to life with a controlling strategy, it can burst out in its natural form.

Code dissolution

If the moral code spontaneously dissolves of its own accord, then morals die without new ones being born. The behavioural guidelines set out in a moral code that tell one 'how to live and what to do in the world' can be seen to be diminishing. Because the dissolution of the code is spontaneous, there is no control over the death of morals. The reference pointer to what is 'good', 'bad', 'right' or 'wrong' disappears. This happening holds the potential to unlock the door of moral imprisonment. With no reference to the 'correct' way to behave, the group chant is forgotten, and the possibility of singing one's own song emerges.

With no moral code ruling over one's actions, events outside one's known remit or structure are permissible. Anything can happen without resistance. The constraints that a moral code puts upon happenings are hefty. One must always be on the lookout for 'dangerous' happenings that are recognized by the code as being 'bad' or 'wrong'. When the moral code dissolves, there are no such warnings of unpredictable events. There is no longer a protective barrier of morals that steers us clear from something that we have been taught is 'bad'. At last, all is down to us. The shackles of taught behaviour tumble. We have nothing to fall back on to tell us what is 'right' or 'wrong'. The heart reclaims its role as a guide. Our behaviour reflects this accordingly, gradually loosening itself from the ingrained habits of restraint and resistance. Every behaviour is accepted and given an airing. The relief and refreshment of this is wonderful. To be released from the confines of morals is to taste life as you always knew it could be but could not relax enough to experience.

When, and if, this happens is independent of choice, will or control. To accept the uncontrollability of this release is to surrender to the possibility of it never happening. Full acceptance results in the extinction of the need for it to happen.

As the moral code disintegrates, behaviour can happen without the intervention of moral judgement. The persuasion of others to adhere to what is 'right' or 'best' holds no sticking power. This may result in a breakaway from those humans that profess the profanity of such a disregard of their moral code. Drifting from the community, lovers, colleagues and friends can be a by-product. No longer constrained by the forces of ancestral 'control', one stands at the threshold to 'freedom'. The chance to 'sing your own song' is alive. This standing at the threshold comes with a wonderful sense of bewilderment. As the moral structure is lost, so too is the struggle to keep living within moral confines. The problems associated with continually breaking the code vanish.

With the spontaneous breakdown of the moral code and surrender to the outcomes of that breakdown, the potential for singing one's own song is glimpsed. The heart that previously filtered isness by selecting parts of it that felt most comfortable, whilst rejecting the uncomfortable parts, now blossoms in the openness of indifference. The openness lets everything into and out of the heart without discrimination. This includes the backlog of emotions and experiences that were previously shut out and judged to be 'bad'. Two common elements that get backlogged are fear and pain. Anything that causes fear or pain can be closed-off through the effort of non-acceptance. That pain and fear are healthy experiences is denied and this denial creates a hardened exterior around the heart in the form of a tense body, stuck feelings, and dogmatic belief systems. This protection from fear and pain serves to provide the appearance of separation from those aspects of life. The self then appears to be isolated from isness. In closing off from fear and pain, we close off to all aspects of life. In creating an apparent separation from isness, the self is in effect saying 'isness is not good enough and can be bettered'. Of course, the irony of this viewpoint is that even if there were less pain and fear in isness, it would still be isness. If the need to better isness disintegrates, then one can open up to the healing process of letting the fears and pain of the past express themselves. The heart is thereby given the space to express fully through the mind, body and emotions.

With this, the alienated part of us, which we tried to isolate by closing our heart, reunites. At the absolution of an open heart is the unity of self with isness. This is the absorption of self into isness without a struggle on the part of the self to claim independence from it. The self is always in union with isness yet to honour this is to open-heartedly remain absorbed in it as being *who you are*, without the need to change it.

Dancing to the song

When we sing our own song, instead of the group chant of learned morals, we are essentially dying in our personal direction and being reborn in our heart's direction. To sing our song is to let the voice of the heart be heard clearly and to respond to it by dancing. This is the dance of ease. The more we respond to the voice of our heart, the more we give up unnecessary control mechanisms and let life live itself. This gives the appearance that life is getting easier. However, life is always easy. It is only the effort to make it into something complex that gives it the appearance of difficulty.

When the moral code disintegrates, no new morals are being born, and there is a lack of guidance. There is no human support, as new morals cannot be successfully absorbed from another. The structure of the code is falling apart and there is no way to rebuild it. Without moral guidance, the 'right' way to go is unknown. There is no longer any 'best' way to go about life. To dance to the song is to follow the heart instead of following morals. In following the heart, one firstly hears the voice of what seems to be an individual heart. Honouring this heart, one recognizes that it is not owned. Then the recognition that it is the *one heart* is possible. The difference between the heart and isness dissolves, and they are seen as one and the same.

This dance of ease is a wondrous enjoyment of isness. Life is a celebration on every level. Pleasure and comfort still remain as preferences of the mind, emotions, and physical body, yet the 'person' who used to prefer pleasure and comfort to pain and discomfort has dissolved. They have been absorbed into isness and are no longer trying to be distinct from *all that is*. With such a surrender, the self is recognised as having always been absorbed in isness. Attempts to be different from isness are given up and ironically, in doing so, the full uniqueness of one's own personal song can flow forth. When we give up trying to make our self unique by using intellectual, emotional or physical strategies, then we unleash the potential to sing our own song based on the recognition of our essential unity.

With no moral reference point, life is 'free' to flow in any direction, in any way. Life is *always* this way, however the act of moral referencing can cloud this recognition and lead to denial. Without a moral guide, the flow of ease takes us toward our heart's direction. When we dance to the song of our heart, we do *what we love*, not what is expected of us. Once our own moral code has collapsed, we are no longer obliged to satisfy others' codes. We then do not have a directional flow that moves in accordance with what is 'right'. We can *be who we are* instead of trying to be 'right' or 'good'. In total acceptance of who we are, there is no need to *change anything*. Although things naturally continue changing, our need to urgently grasp that change and manipulate it for our own means diminishes. This is rest. This is the cessation of struggle.

Ease of life

Once one is dancing to the song of the heart, certain differences become apparent. With the heart as a guide and the once-stringent authority of morals absent, *ease* takes the place of moral authority.

The heart is an honourable expression of isness when there is no attempt to greedily gain something for one's 'self'. By innocently following the heart, we find that ease takes precedence where once morals ruled. Flowing in this way, without resistance, we are drawn toward *that which is easy*. When we wholly surrender to our heart's directive without excessive concern for 'personal' loss or gain, then our whole life is recognized as being easy. Life is easy. It lives itself whether or not we interfere with the process.

To make life difficult takes tremendous effort. It is the effort to 'get' something that makes life appear difficult. Humans engineer this complexity. It is a perception that grapples with isness. Simplicity is a resting without the need for the difficulty of complexity. To follow the song of the heart is to honour the simplicity of life. This can manifest on the physical plane as a relaxation of the attachment to objects. It can manifest emotionally as a letting be of any emotion that comes so that none are stored up. It can manifest in the mind as a calming of the erratic thought-patterns that disturb the balance of the body and emotions. Once difficulty has ceased, simplicity may manifest in various ways. One major way is that day-to-day situations are *accepted*. The need to change isness dissolves and this in itself can reawaken the respect of the ease of life.

Loss of learnt purpose

To sing one's own song is to surrender to the honouring of isness. This surrender is extremely attractive, yet a great loss accompanies it: the loss of purpose.

When your life is lived with a meaning and a purpose that is given by the community, then this limits your personal existence. It narrows down the possibilities of living your life from your heart as opposed to living it according to learnt values. Meaning and purpose dictate that a certain direction must be taken. If this direction is not the way of the heart, then it is ultimately dissatisfying. Even if the desires of a learnt purpose are met, they cannot bring the contentment that comes from following one's heart.

With surrendered control, life is lived without the imposition of a meaning or purpose. Isness is allowed to move without the intervention of a person. A person with a meaning or purpose for life will naturally intervene on the flow that naturally occurs within isness. When traced to the root, this meaning or purpose is inherited from parents, teachers, communities or religion. To live life with a learnt purpose is to live life with someone else's purpose.

People often base the purpose of their lives upon the solving of problems. Problems can give a sense of importance to one's 'self' and one's life. They can also be used to maintain and nurture a sense of purpose. The conquest of problems can become a reason to exist. When such a challenge presents itself, life becomes a series of solutions to self-invented problems. The purpose of life becomes the solution of the next problem. Intellectualism, being an advanced capacity to formulate verbal ideas, can be used to create problems. The intellectual can calculate sophisticated problems for their life. The very same intellect can be used functionally in an effortless, problem-free life. It is simply a difference of style.

When the moral code disintegrates, the importance of judgements and analyses diminish. Worries about problems, and the problems themselves, disappear. And with them disappears the purpose of solving those problems. With the invention of problems ceasing, the purpose of overcoming problems is redundant. If problems are given up, then the believed 'cause' of a problem need no longer be aggressively tackled and may even become useful.

A faith or doctrine that tells us why we exist or what is the 'right' way to live has very little impact on existence as a whole. Existence carries on with or without these interpretations of 'reality'. When we honour the nature of existence by likewise carrying on without obsessive interpretation, then we can recognize our 'selves' as *being isness*. We exist *as* existence when we cease to struggle with it.

Along with a loss of purpose and a resulting lack of direction, one whose moral code has disintegrated may be struck by confusion. Mixed with a serene enjoyment of new-found 'freedom', this can take the form of bewilderment. The surrender to this bewildering release from limitation can in itself seem confusing. Nothing matters anymore, nor does anything *have* to be done. There is no mission and no causes to fight for. There are no motives and no persistent struggle. Life is for isness. It is simply to be what is. No meaning, no purpose, no interpretation.

With no moral reference, there is no concern about the style of one's behaviour or the outcome of it. All can be as it is. No emotional uprising needs to be stopped or changed. With this acceptance, there is a resting. The struggle is over, and purpose lost. New vistas of opportunities continually present themselves. With so much unlimited movement, the action of choice can seem bewildering. To choose when there is no motive can appear impossible. However, in the cessation of struggle, one learns to surrender to isness by letting any need for *certainty* die. Everything is allowed to take its course. This is what is *happening already*. Everything is already taking its course. To honour this happening is to let the flow of existence take us where it does, without any interference on our part to 'better' the situation or by trying to seize 'control'.

Like a little beetle that you stand on and squash upon the pavement, our own physical lives will spontaneously and uncontrollably shift realms. At the moment of impact, as our bodies die, all struggle will be recognized as futile. To recognize it in a living body is to allow struggle to die. With no struggle, our self-important problems will fade and a trouble-free, purposeless existence opens up for us. From this base, our purpose can renew itself as a simple honouring of our open heart's direction.

Guilt dissolved

With no sense of moral value, guilt can dissolve to be replaced with a sense of excitement at the vastness of isness. Guilt derives from a feeling of obligation, a feeling that one is responsible beyond one's control. If we try to be responsible for events that are out of our hands, then we can carry the burden of guilt. If we can deeply accept all our actions as being conditioned, then we do not hold our influence as being so important in the scheme of things. Guilt is a compounding sense of worry that one has done the 'wrong' or 'worst' thing. It manifests in the physical body and in the emotions. It is often accompanied by remorse, which is a self-pitying sadness that looks mournfully upon the 'wrong' action.

When the emotions are 'freed', they can spontaneously flow forth. With no interference from the mental vehicle, emotions that once depended on thought to prolong their expression can now quickly and efficiently express themselves and then dissipate. Twinges of guilt can be an emotional response to moral judgements held in the mind. With the disintegration of the moral code, the judgement process does not exist as a guide. Actions are not prevented or encouraged using the mechanisms of 'right' or 'wrong', 'good' or 'bad'. These mechanisms may exist as a *mental process* but they are not allowed to interfere with life's 'choices'. Such is the release when interference from a moral code ceases.

Lack of familiar reference

The breakdown of the moral construct leaves a startlingly stark space that was once filled with the conventions of 'bad' and 'good', 'right' and 'wrong'. The spontaneous dissolution of the code results in the death of morals with no new ones to replace them. This breath-taking occurrence can happen instantly or gradually but the result is the same: there is no longer a reference point for 'what to do' and 'how to do it'. The moral code imprinted on the mind no longer serves as a guide and the bewilderment of infinite options is both awesome and disconcerting. Such a loss can be uncomfortable. As with all loss, there can be the recognition that the thing that was 'lost' was *never owned*. With the loss of anything, the lamentation of seeing its own autonomy is coupled with the heart-breaking lack of a reliable replacement. We depended on something that is inevitably transitory. So it is with the moral code. When it disintegrates, there is no immediate replacement for its function. If there is an *openness to be* in this awesome, uncomfortable lack of reference then the potential of our own song beckons us.

Everyone has had a glimpse of a situation in which no guidance or reference exists. It is a space where we are able to see clearly our own innate uniqueness of form. To unfailingly recognize this is to relax into *being unique within that which is the same*. However, there is a learnt reaction deterring the one who has no moral reference from simply being without it: the fear of the unknown. This can arise and motivate the individual to urgently seek guidance. Then begins the effort to replace their devastated moral code with a new one. The hope exists that somehow, somewhere, someone can provide what has startlingly been lost. The urgency is motivated by the feeling that life may soon take an irrecoverable turn into a dissolution of bondage, and the self will be absorbed into isness. With this absorption comes the loss of that which was once treasured: self-importance, status, purpose, problems, and struggle.

The seeming safety of a strictly enforced moral code may be yearned for once it is missing. So begins the search to 'return' to the 'right way to be' without any reference to what 'right' is. Here lies the temptation of aspiration. It is the temptation to find a guru, teacher or religious figure that embodies a way of being that is attractive, and to aspire to live the same way. This gives a semblance of hope where there is none. A glimmering of opportunity arises. Having lost one's whole meaning, purpose and self-important direction in life, the chance to begin again from scratch can present itself in the form of a guru's doctrine or a religious teaching. Many of these teachings are ironically pointing at how to achieve the complete dissolution of bondage through the attainment of 'freedom' or 'enlightenment'. However, the urge to be free reinforces the sense of bondage. The very wish for enlightenment is a denial of our nature as being enlightened. The one who is enlightened knows that they were never unenlightened; therefore it is impossible to *become* enlightened. Enlightenment is only of interest for those who still believe that they can become enlightened.

When you hope that new doctrines can guide you, then the attachment to these doctrines can result in the writing of a new moral code. Following a teaching can therefore become a prison in itself while masquerading as a healthy way to rebuild your life. Only when the spontaneous, unaided dissolution of the moral code is accompanied by an openness to *any and all* possible results of never having it back again, can you be as we are without denial or control. Any effort to control the uncontrollable is a struggle that denies your inherent nature.

Following the spontaneous dissolution of moral structure, this struggle can cease and can stay that way unless there is a concerted effort to take it up again. A return to struggle may be encouraged by the lure of familiarity that takes the form of a safe place filled with problems, challenges, difficulties and therefore a new learnt purpose.

There is no support in the bewildering emptiness that lies in the disintegration of the moral code. When the nature of being is revealed in surrender it is seen to be unsupported. In the honour of our nature, we are unsupported. In opening to this amazing void, the very fabric of existence shows itself to be *without the need for meaning*.

Echoes of patterns

Even when the moral code has completely dissolved, it can echo itself in one's behaviour. The moral code and one's behaviour patterns emerge simultaneously. They are both conditioned. The moral code writes itself with adjustment from behavioural trial and error. When your action oversteps other's moral boundaries, they impose their moral code on you. In this way, behavioural experiments test the boundaries of others. Their subsequent projection of 'where the boundaries lie' constructs the moral code. Likewise, the moral code adjusts behaviour. It is used as a reference point to gauge the 'right' or 'best' way to go about life. Dancing together in this synergy, the moral code and one's behaviour patterns stimulate and nurture one another.

When the code dies, momentum within the behaviour patterns can continue. The behaviour, having been influenced for so long by the moral code, continues to resemble reference to it *without* referring to it. For example, if you prevented yourself from showing anger because your moral code said so, then you may continue to behave in this way after the moral code has disintegrated. Although you are no longer referring to the moral code as to how to behave in a situation in which you feel angry, your behaviour continues to be similar due to the conditioning of it. The pattern of preventing the expression of anger continues through the momentum of conditioning. Judgements remain as natural mental functions and have been conditioned by the teaching of a moral code. However this function *is no longer taken as a reference point* as to how to live one's life. It has lost its role as a guide, yet continues to function through momentum. The moment it is referred to again as a guide, then the moral code is being re-established. Even if there is a rewriting of the moral code, if there is an acceptance of this rewriting then the struggle is not present and the moral code has no more opportunity for growth. Acceptance is an absence of urgent effort to change anything. All is as it is without it needing to change. Acceptance does not need to prevent anything from being 'wrong' or 'bad', and does not need to encourage anything because it is 'right' or 'good'.

The infinite options

For the one who experiences the destruction of moral confines, a grand secret of infinite options is revealed. The revelation that there are infinite options in one's life is coupled with the recognition that this is the case for everyone, even those still living within a moral code. The only restriction for those still struggling is that they deny their own potential by sticking as best as they can to their moral code. The moral code therefore filters the infinite options that exist and make it appear as if there is limited choice. After all, choosing with reference to a moral code means choosing what is 'right' and 'good' while avoiding what is 'wrong' and 'bad'.

To be in the annihilation of moral values is to cease using mental judgements of one's actions to modify behaviour. With no moral structure to restrict behaviour, the infinite options are revealed and the mind, body and emotion take command of behaviour choices. The body chooses *for the body* according to its conditioning and genetic make-up. The mind and emotions also choose by themselves for themselves according to conditioning and without moral intervention. This is when the body, mind and emotions come into their own. No longer restricted in their expression by a persistent attempt to keep them under control, they are free to spread out into the universe in the way that they inherently know is best. Choices are so spontaneous that they can hardly be called 'choices' any more. 'Happenings' is more fitting. Life reveals itself to be a series of happenings. Conditioned responses abound, unpolluted by judgement, analysis and the intellectual regime of moral enforcement. Nothing is set in stone anymore. Anything can happen. This is always the case, yet it is only the disintegration of the moral code accompanied by an honour of isness that leads to this recognition.

Infinite options are available to us in our individual lives. Personal choices can be made to determine where we live, who we spend time with, what we eat, what work we do, how we spend our leisure time, how we dress and all other details of day-to-day life. Such choices are made under the influence of conditioning. When our conditioning becomes totally aligned with our heart, then individual choices are made from the heart and not according to the learnt values of others. Life is an open game. Every direction undertaken is an open invitation to explore. When this is honoured, the attitude is that *anything can happen*; therefore whatever does happen is not struggled with. Without this honour, the limitation of options creates a struggle when the happenings of isness do not fit within the expected limitations.

Of course, we cannot choose everything. Those aspects of existence that are outside of our choice are determined by destiny. The weather is an example of this. Destiny also moves in our personal lives. When our heart chooses for us, then individual choice and destiny are aligned, and events seem to happen 'as they should'. They happen at the 'right time' and in the 'right place'. Auspicious coincidences abound. Personal choice and destiny become one and the same. Once the moral code has disintegrated, our conditioning moves unhindered by intellectual judgment. Being moved by destiny is therefore easier, as we are no longer fighting the flow of it. We can accept what destiny brings and the choices that our heart makes for us. This acceptance is the honouring of *no bondage*. With the honouring that there is - and never was - any bondage, then 'freedom' is impossible to attain and contentment can take the place of the struggle for elusive freedom. The honour of no bondage brings the recognition and acceptance that bondage was self-invented by a will to control isness. This will to control made an agenda out of bettering isness, and it is only when this agenda is completely given up that we can honour isness as it is without wanting to change it.

Using teachers to rebuild the code

Once the moral code has been lost, a conscious decision to have it rewritten by new authorities may be made. Restructuring association with others to include new friends, teachers, lovers, and religions can bring with it the opportunity to have new influences in one's life. These new influences are consciously chosen teachers. The one who has lost their moral code selects these teachers because they wish to rebuild it. As the morals of the old code die, new ones are born from the moral codes of these teachers. A fresh inheritance of 'how to be in this world' is transferred.

The motive to seek a teacher in this way may be rooted in loneliness. The one whose morals have dissolved may feel split off from the group chant, and may pine for social or emotional intimacy with others. The wish to be with others who have been, or are, in this daunting and exciting place can take the individual into a group under a teacher's guidance. Like swimming in cold water, knowing that each other is there can make the ordeal feel more comfortable.

The aspiration towards a teacher can result in an attempt to mimic their behaviour. This re-establishes a new moral code. Trying to adjust one's behaviour to match another's is futile. It cannot be done successfully and it requires the effort to deny one's own natural pulls. The constant repression of one's own unique expression in an attempt to correspond with another's behaviour is a continual source of frustration. Although the behaviour pattern of a teacher may be aspired to, that pattern cannot be replicated in anyone else. Everybody's behaviour patterns are unique. Attempting to recreate another's behaviour patterns can drain one of energy and annihilate the capacity to honour one's expression. Tired and un-successful, we find that this is the perfect place to give up the search.

A teacher can be useful in this capacity: to provide an unsuccessful method or to be a reference point of aspira-tion that cannot be mimicked. A seeker can then make effort around a teacher until the frustration of failure is so great that every teaching, method, aspiration, hope and moral is abandoned as absurd and useless. 'The search' is then over. Indeed, the most potent teacher is one who does not rekindle the dying embers of hope by presenting a new moral code. A potent teacher will give no basis for a reconstruction of identity. No prescriptive measure will be given. A potent teacher knows the effect that prescription will have on an eager seeker. Without prescription, the seeker has nothing to do, and no way do it. There is no help in resurrecting their moral code. The code is allowed to die. In this space the heart can burst forth and take its original place as guide of their life.

Without the direction of an authority, desperation may overcome a seeker. The turning to a source of authority in a teacher leaves the teacher in a very powerful position. The seeker wants so much for a teacher to have the answers, and there are many teachers who want to claim that they have them. The teacher may be motivated by their own need to convince others that their beliefs are 'real', thereby reinforcing that they are 'right'. Any teacher who is carrying their own moral code will stimulate in the seeker the desire to move within moral confines. The teacher and the seeker both play the game in which the belief is held that the teacher 'knows best'. This is comfortable for both. Both have their roles and neither is confused about who 'knows best'. The teacher may morally disallow himself or herself the option of 'not knowing', so that they then have the 'answer to everything'.

Yet, the entirety of isness cannot be known. We can only be it. Knowing needs an object and a subject. If we know something, there is a knower knowing the known. However, in simply being, the subject and object merge. If we are being something, the 'be-er' and the 'been' are not separate, they are the same. In being, there is no knowing, for there is no separation and no need to know. Knowing is only useful if we claim to be separate from isness, and wish to reintegrate ourselves with it through intimacy. The game of teacher and disciple supposes that the teacher is fully integrated in isness. Yet the contradiction in this game may be that while the teacher claims to 'know best', he is at the same time supposedly inhabiting a state where knowing is redundant.

The seeker is looking for a guide to give them a map. The map, the seeker hopes, will tell them how to achieve their aspirations by giving them a new moral code to live by. The teacher represents the achievement of the seeker's aspirations. They have trodden the ground. They can show the way. The belief is that the teacher has something that can be given to seeker. If the teacher believes that they have something to give, then the domination-submission game of 'knowing' and 'not knowing' can commence. The seeker believes that they do not 'know' but that the teacher does, that they are not 'free' or 'enlightened' but that the teacher is. Such beliefs can distance both teacher and seeker from the nature of being. Being is independently enlightened. Who is there to get enlightened? Being is unbound. Where is freedom when there is no bondage?

With such constricting beliefs in the attainment of freedom and enlightenment, the nature of *who we are* is not honoured. One's song is stifled, traded in for someone else's. This can seem like a refreshing change from the group chant of non-seekers, yet it is simply a different tone of group chant, that of the seekers.

The consciously selected teacher can provide an example of the possibility of functioning without problems, worries, or moral struggle. For the seeker, seeing that the teacher remains living in the world after the shattering dissolution of life purpose can be a great source of inspiration. A teacher's greatest teachings are in their approach to life, reflected in their mental, emotional and physical behaviour. Any prescriptive remedies issued by a teacher only serve to strengthen or recreate the moral code. Simply being with a potent teacher is far more helpful. It is the recognition that if someone else lost so much of what is commonly valued and lives a life of ease and enjoyment as a result, then anyone can.

The death of blockage

The teacher may be helpful in the area of emotional, mental and physical cleansing. The teacher may not only take the form of another person, but can be a psychoactive substance or a meditation technique. Whether it is looking to another human, ingesting a psychoactive plant or using a meditation method, the seeker is grasping for a way to be. To grasp in this way is to dishonour one's own nature whilst one seeks to recognize it.

Everyone is being all the time. The only variety is in whether or not this is recognized and honoured. The attempts of the seeker to attain something that they inherently *are* can lead them to the necessary therapy in the form of a teacher. Therapy can remove the blocks that distract from the recognition and subsequent honour of our nature. With mental, emotional and physical blockage, the seeker can get caught continually clearing these blocks and this clearance becomes their life purpose. A teacher, drug or technique can help clear the blockage only if there is an acceptance of death. To clear problems up is to allow them to die, not to solve them or fix them. Solving problems only creates more problems. Solutions need problems, and so do those who are applying solutions. A solver will invent problems in order to perpetuate their life purpose. If there is a wish to better one's life through a further sophistication of the moral code, then a teacher, drug or technique will not provide useful therapy. A death of unnecessary burdens *is* useful. Such a death is related to the breakdown of the moral code, not just a restructuring or a refining of it. As the burdens of problems, worries, struggle, frustration, and non-acceptance die, then the moral code disintegrates. 'Rights' and 'wrongs' have less meaning and less impact on one's lifestyle. The infinite options begin to open up. To recognize the infinite options is to allow all distracting blockages to die in their own way and in their own time.

Pushing blockages away does not work and only serves to reinforce them through involvement with them. Death needs no involvement. It happens spontaneously. To attempt to bring about the dying process of blockages is to postpone that very death. Involvement attaches one to the blockage and makes it important. This can result in a reluctance to allow the blockage to die. A fondness can grow for the blockage. Letting go of fondness for blockage has to happen in order to let it die simply. Otherwise, a deep sense of emotional trauma is experienced as the blockage is held onto as a part of the self. There is a struggle as the blockage begins to die but continues to be held onto. A simple death is one where there is acceptance without the need for involvement.

The teacher, drug or technique presents a *form* that may be mistaken as the 'source' of the death experience. Upon the death of blockage, there can be an attachment to that form, and the misconception that the form is the dying process itself. The form may facilitate and support the death of blockage, resulting in a recognition of one's inherent nature, yet it is not the death itself. Death is independent of any happening or action. It does not rely on anyone, any time, any place, or any experience. Isness can be honoured and death can be accepted. This is our natural state. It is the giving up of all effort to remove our selves from isness. We cannot do this. It is as a flower opens or a rock falls to the sea. It happens when it happens.

Any happening that nurtures the death of blockage is a catalyst towards recognising one's own nature. Any attempt to escape isness is a denial of one's nature *as* isness. It is a non-acceptance of *that which is*. This is a struggle that can be prompted by any moral code. If there is a 'right' way to behave then anything conflicting with this learnt code causes tension. Even trying to escape this tension is a struggle. Only the breakdown of the moral code will release the tension caused by the contradiction between actual behaviour and the 'right' way to behave.

The search

The resurrection of the moral code is made possible by the 'search'. This commonly takes the form of a doctrine to be followed or a teacher to aspire to. Many teachers offer the opportunity of salvation through various disciplines and approaches. Most of them are based on the teacher's own attempts at achieving 'freedom' or 'enlightenment'. Prescriptions are given out based on what *seemed* to help the teacher achieve their aim. The one who recognizes their innate nature need not ask questions about it, whereas the one who denies their innate nature will digest a multitude of answers. However, anyone giving serious advice to others as to how to reach a certain state of 'freedom' or 'enlightenment' is denying the innate characteristics of isness. 'Freedom' only exists where there is bondage. 'Enlightenment' only exists where there is ignorance. To quest for 'freedom' or 'enlightenment', or to help others in their quest, is to perpetuate the complementary halves of bondage and ignorance. The wish to be free is itself bondage. The wish to be enlightened is ignorance.

The paradox of 'the search' is that what is being sought is *isness*. Since there is nothing outside of isness, 'the search' is geared toward a closer sense of intimacy with isness. Yet, even intimacy with isness would suggest a separation from it. We are isness, and there is no escaping it. We can attempt to detach into the realm of self-importance where the self is perceived as not only being distinct from isness but also superior to it. But even this realm is part of isness. The only 'teacher' we can rest in is isness. Honouring our nature as *being isness* heralds the end of 'the search'. It is the total loss of a personal agenda designed to better what is. It is the falling into the heart, and the falling into acceptance.

However, 'the search' may be perpetuated by the appearance of needs. Needing an authority figure is a strong imprint. When there is nothing left, no reference point, no parent, teacher or elder to advise 'how to' or 'what to', a strong vacuum of authority arises. Here lies the potential to *become* that vacuum, to *be* without authority. Yet, the conditioned response of fear can nullify this vast opportunity. Instead of the dissolution of the self into isness, there can be a fight for survival, to maintain self-importance. A teacher on a crusade of any kind can support this re-emergence of struggle. They can offer a plan, a way to 'get better'. This can again trigger the denial of isness and encourage a long-winded fight to 'return'. The excessive irony of searching is that there is nowhere to return to. Isness can never be left at all. All that can happen is that an honour of isness replaces the denial of it. There is nothing new to 'become'. Only a change of approach is possible, and this is a result of chance, rather than of doing.

During the search, the distractions of having multiple life purposes can detract from focusing one's life-purpose onto the search. To have focus on only one purpose is to refine the purpose of life. When all life is for is to attain freedom, self-realisation or enlightenment, then the recognition that there is nothing to attain can occur. The goal of freedom, self-realisation or enlightenment is always bound to failure. We cannot become what we inherently are. There can only be the simple recognition that we were always this way. When this is recognized, the efforts made during the search can seem ironic and sometimes humorous. All effort to be is futile. The push to get into a permanent state of freedom, bliss or enlightenment can only end in failure. Any 'state' is transitory. The urgent effort to perpetuate a state is frustrating. Since the way isness flows is in constant change, anything gained must also be lost. Even the peace, relaxation or well-being experienced in a meeting with a teacher, a drug experience or a meditation technique will dissipate. Everlasting peace is only possible if it is not sought for. It cannot be got, it cannot be bought, and it cannot be inherited. It can only be recognized as a cessation of an unnecessary struggle, a struggle that was compounded by the search for peace. The unity of isness that we all are can be honoured only when we give up the search to get something.

Any place, any time

Happenings are merely a characteristic of isness. All actions are isness. Your 'self' is isness. The meltdown of boundaries that block this simple recognition can happen *any time, anywhere*. The methods of studentship, psychoactive plant ingestion, meditation, yoga, tantra, or anything geared towards the elusive 'freedom' can provide 'mystical' out of body experiences, unity and the dissolution of boundaries. These are the glimpses of the dissolution of bondage and the end of struggle. When the experience ends, the boundaries and struggle return. These methods are the domain of the seeker. Simple methods designed to bring about enjoyment such as sport, TV, sex, films, travel, dance, walking and conversation are equally as likely to be engaged in when the glimpse of no-bondage occurs. The seeker filters out the experiences of methods that are not traditionally associated with 'freedom attainment', and focuses heavily on those that are. As a result, the seeker becomes convinced that certain methods bring about 'mystical' experiences. They often become fanatical about them as a way of glimpsing the freedom that is yearned for.

Mystical is simply that which is beyond comprehension. The one whose search has ended simply has experiences. The experiences are not 'mystical' because there is no effort to comprehend them. They spontaneously happen *all the time*. The one whose search has ended does not filter some experiences as being of a 'higher' or 'more profound' quality than others. Having allowed isness to swallow the self up whilst it remains intact, there no longer exists a 'higher' or a 'lower, a 'more profound' or a 'less profound'. Such judgemental reasoning remains only as a function of the mind, and is no longer utilized as a means to look at isness.

Anything may seem helpful to the recognition of our nature as *being*. Ultimately, the recognition is dependent on nothing. It is a simple honouring of our nature *as* being. Any method to 'be', whether it appears to be successful or not, can not induce being. We *are* being. This being is in no way separated from doing. If we 'do' something in order to 'be', then we create a perceived separation between doing and being. The perception is that there is doing followed by being. 'Doing nothing' to 'be' also keeps the distinction there. The perception in this case is that we can 'be' when we are not 'doing'. When we honour the merged nature of being and doing, methods become unimportant. Methods are more enjoyable the less effort we make to gain something from them. For one who is honouring their nature as a simultaneous, continual *being* and *doing* , it is clear that no method can bring about 'being'. Being has no dependence and no time reference, for that is its nature. Therefore, any awakening to the honour of our nature happens independently of circumstance and time.

4 *Struggle*

An attachment to struggle is common. It is like someone who wishes to jump over hurdles rather than have a clear run, because that way they have something to do along the way. Overcoming the hurdles of self-created problems gives life a 'meaning'. This 'meaning' is only the intellectual understanding that life's main activity has become the solving of problems. The fear that the 'meaning of life' will no longer be intellectually understood means that neither problems nor solutions can be surrendered, and the struggle must continue.

Bettering isness

Applying morals can create problems. Something is seen as wrong. It is seen as needing to be corrected. Here the struggle arises as isness is not accepted. If isness needs to change from a moral perspective, then the one who needs to change it has an impossible struggle. Isness cannot be changed. If isness changes, it is still isness. There is no escaping isness. Trying to change it, trying to change our selves, or implementing technologies designed to alleviate the human condition cannot help us to escape isness.

Life is so easy. It lives itself for us. We do not have to struggle through it. The perpetual grasping for a 'better' situation inevitably leads one to a continual disappointment that life is 'just not good enough'. We have no 'right to life'. Life is a gift and it is *what it is*. Accepting this is to ride the 'ups' and 'downs', enjoying both and not insisting on having more of one than the other.

Life is a struggle when we believe ourselves to be more important than the rest of the universe. However, if we give up this exaggerated self-importance and accept isness without wanting to change it, then we witness the ceasing of struggle. There is no way we cannot be isness. Isness is what we are. If we have the experience of being separate from isness, this is only a mask of exaggerated self-importance that clouds clarity. When we surrender whole-heartedly to all that is in the present moment, we effortlessly recognize our nature as being isness.

The struggle of discontentment with isness is ironically stimulated by the effort to get out of the struggle by 'getting something better'. Even if this appears to be achieved, the pattern of 'getting more' remains. The struggle can only cease if this pattern disappears. Yet, even wanting the pattern to disappear is a 'getting more' and is therefore a discontentment with isness. The disappearance of this pattern, and the subsequent cessation of struggle, are both spontaneous happenings and cannot be *done*.

Boundaries

Boundaries are functional. They can mark the edges of territories so that we may act in the world. However, if we invest in boundaries as being the definitive guides to our existence, then we are constrained by them. It is our involvement in boundaries, not the boundaries themselves, that is the constraint. If we utilize boundaries effectively, we recognize them as guides for the world and not strict, rigid walls that restrict us.

We understand isness by splitting it up. Fragmentation is the only way the mind can understand something. Limitation must be employed otherwise the mind cannot grasp it. If a concept has no boundaries then it is lost. The mind simply cannot comprehend the infinite vastness of isness. Finite boundaries are constructed to house concepts and perceptions. We understand to walk through a door, not a wall. We understand where our body ends and the air begins. These perceptions are supported by boundaries and are functional. However, if we invest in actions that are limited by boundaries as the only possible thing that can happen, then the boundaries go beyond function and begin to limit our intimacy with isness.

In isness there is infinite happenings. Anything can happen. Investment in boundaries denies this and distances us from the dance of isness. If we are convinced that because we understand to walk through a door that we can never walk into a wall, then our universe is shrinking, or rather we are shrinking from the universe. If we understand the boundaries of the body, yet invest in them so heavily that we exclude the experience of physically merging with things 'outside' our body, then our experience of existence is again limited. To utilize the functionality of boundaries without trying to distance ourselves from isness through them is to function in the world whilst at the same time honouring our nature as unbounded.

Moral codes are kept in force by boundaries. To keep within the boundary of the code is 'good', while stepping over the boundary is 'bad'. To sing one's own song is to overstep the moral boundaries of others with acceptance. The acceptance negates the need for others to forsake their moral codes. To dance to the song of the heart is to warmly disregard whether the steps of the dance are different from or similar to others. All is allowed.

The collapse of boundaries is aided by the cessation of problem invention. When the overstepping of a moral boundary is a problem, then that serves to keep the boundary in place. When the overstepping of moral boundaries is no longer a problem, the boundaries can die.

When a moral code disintegrates, the code *appears* to still be in place until the boundaries of it are crossed. When the dead boundaries of the now disintegrated code are crossed, there is the recognition that the boundary is not there. With this recognition, there is no problem stepping over this imaginary mark. However, if the code remains intact, the crossing of boundaries will be a frustrating problem and will reinforce the code with guilt, regret and struggle.

The struggle to stay within boundaries is an attempt to 'control' the uncontrollable. It is as if the struggling human is in a huge meadow of infinite proportions, yet they are convinced that an invisible force field surrounds them, fencing them into a small area. Every time the force field is crossed, the struggling human reacts by claiming that they must stay inside it. Despite their efforts, however, they continue to breach their imaginary boundaries and become tired by the punishment that they dole out to themselves. This is followed by an even greater effort to stay within the boundaries, which leads to further tired-ness. In such a state of retention and denial, the struggling human can give up the enjoyment of being in the meadow, instead concentrating on the continual battle to keep within invented confines.

Once the moral code has disintegrated, even the habitual act of keeping within the boundaries is not a problem, even though one recognizes that they are not there. There is an acceptance that this is a dying habit. As there is no longer a 'right' way to be, the apparent contradiction of recognizing our unbounded nature and yet habitually staying within boundaries does not create struggle. If there are no morals, then the momentum of continuing to act within the boundaries of a dead moral code is accepted and not acted upon as 'wrong' or 'bad'.

Need for change

To better your personal life through improvements is a totally natural urge. An open heart will flow through the mind, body and emotions, responding to their desires and making them more healthy and powerful. Bettering the whole of isness, on the other hand, is a sign of discontentment. Bettering everything that exists by somehow trying to inflate your personal life so that it becomes bigger than everything else put together not only sacrifices your sense of perspective but inevitably ends in failure and frustration.

If you consider yourself to be more important than isness, then you will be motivated to make an effort to 'better isness'. Self-important humans insist that such an effort makes a difference to result. They put themselves at the centre of a cause-and-effect scenario. Causes are of the human imagination. When a person imagines himself or herself to be the cause, this breeds exaggerated self-importance. Someone making an effort to better their life will be proud if isness happens to correspond with their efforts and be disappointed and frustrated if it does not.

Ironically, when things are to be made 'better', they are straight away made 'worse'. If this were not so, they could not be made 'better'. One that is continually pursuing the 'good' or the 'heavenly', creates the 'bad' or the 'hellish' around them. For nothing can become good unless it is something different from 'good'. Therefore 'bad' must be invented in order to sustain a purpose that says 'I am here to make things better'.

The struggle to make things better is quite distinct from responding to the desires of the mind, emotions and physical body. The three components of mind, emotions (or feelings) and physical body make up our expressive vehicles. They are the vehicles with which our heart expresses itself. They are our contact with the planet, with each other, and with all things. The vehicles have desires that arise from this contact. When our heart responds to these desires, we answer the call of these expressive vehicles. A heart that is not greedy will not be obsessed with the fulfilment of these desires, but will move easily towards fulfilment and find it if it is *easy*. If fulfilment is not easy, then the heart will accept the non-fulfilment. With an open heart's response to the expressive vehicles, there is no attempt to 'better' isness. There is simply a natural movement towards fulfilment to see if it is easy to find. Struggle is absent because *the result is not attached to*. Fulfilment or non-fulfilment is equally acceptable.

The cessation of effort and the subsequent loss of struggle beckon an unimaginably restful state, a state in which the 'trying human' no longer remains. The fear of such a death keeps the self-important human running on the wheel of effort. The human that is intent on 'bettering' isness faces a constant stream of challenges. These challenges are jading and tiring yet they are relished as they maintain a sense of purpose. With this comes a 'safety' from the 'threat' of death.

Death

Death is an absence. We relate death to departure and loss. It is an emptiness of what is commonly perceived as the fullness of life. However, the emptiness that death represents is an integral part of life. When we reconnect with this emptiness, it can be experienced as a void. All things cease. There is no activity and no separation, and because of this there is no stillness and no unity. It is simply a void of that with which we are familiar. Yet, this is also a very familiar space as we have all been there.

It is the disconnection from this void that causes the startling mistrust of death. When we allow the void to be part and parcel of daily living, then death takes on a new flavour. It is experienced as a daily transition of death and renewal.

We are constantly in this process of death and renewal. Change is the only continuum. For the one who is not in denial of this change, death and birth are the same – there cannot be one without the other. This process of decay and renewal *is* life. All follows this protean flow. To hold onto one's self, and to attempt to protect it from this flow of change, is gross denial.

To betray our nature in such a way can result in a struggle that may only appear to end upon physical death. The final collapse of the physical body heralds a letting go in the material plane. What happens thereafter is speculative and open to learnt philosophy and opinion. The wish to know about what happens after physical death is a distraction from experiencing the void. Theories and philosophies can be enjoyed but to invest in any of them as holding the 'answer' to what happens after physical death merely reveals that the question was being asked urgently enough to invent an 'answer' from a rich array of ideas.

When we see that the process of death and birth is the nature of life, then the holding onto life as an unchanging phenomena seems absurd. All will come to pass. Understanding this can give peace of mind, while recognizing and embracing this deep in the heart can release us from the limitations that accompany fear and mistrust of death.

The saviours

The attempt to change the world outside is often a subconscious attempt to change it inside. One can take on the ordeals of the world as a distraction from one's own ordeals. Saintliness, along with the 'good' intentions that go with it, then turns into a search to find something or someone that is 'worse off' than oneself. This search is motivated by the hope that finding one 'worse off' will give one an inner satisfaction of being 'better off' which in turn will fill a gap. This gap is a yearning to *be* without struggle. To struggle on someone else's behalf can give the appearance of the cessation of one's own struggle. In the intense effort to help another, one's own problems are in the background. This may be sustained for some time, yet inevitably a problem will surface. So continues the cycle of being a struggling saviour. A new external problem must be sought to assuage the problem inside. This is a 'life mission' or purpose. This kind of saviour must create 'bad' situations in order that they might make them better.

The struggling saviour is propelled onwards by the teaching that we are to 'do something with our lives', that we 'should make something out of our lives'. This moral teaching causes us to fear a life without recognition. To be unrecognized would be a strong reminder that our importance is equal in relation to isness, and not greater. The will to be recognized is a protective strategy designed to 'keep safe' a perception of exaggerated self-importance. To let this self-importance crumble is to accept our equality among isness and give up the deep need to be recognized. Our lives are then 'free' to weave any pattern without our holding to the pattern prescribed to us by others. With an uncontrolled unleashing of the heart's responses, life becomes an unpredictable adventure full of wonder and awe. This is so effortless. The effort we make to have an openly singing heart simply closes it. *We do not have to do a thing* to appreciate the amazing, delicious qualities of life. There is nothing we *have* to do. There is simply response. We can respond to our surroundings without any effort.

Someone who is not struggling with a sense of lack within themselves does not need to do acts of helping for recognition or in an attempt to feel whole. They have healed themselves first before facilitating the healing of others and can therefore act out of selfless compassion. The saving acts are not loaded with self-concern but are rather directed straight from an open heart. Such saviours are very effective and can make a lasting, beneficial impact on the lives of others. Their absence of internal struggle means that they do not rely on helping the struggles of others as a way to feel intimate with isness. An effective saviour has released such internal struggle and can fully enjoy the experience of being absorbed in isness. Such joy naturally overflows into the world around them as a contribution towards others. There is an effortless ease about such a contribution for it is simply a sharing of their experience of a unified existence brimming with love and joy. Since the whole of existence is a 'sharing', we do not need to try to share. Effort in sharing is self-important sacrifice and has an element of greed. Effortless sharing is a simple enjoyment of love and a celebration of the sheer vastness that is who we are.

Desire hierarchies and compassion

Constantly putting the desires of another before your own is self-importance. Constantly putting your own desires before that of another's is also self-importance. The former claims that another is more worthy, the latter claims that you are more worthy. Whether you demote or promote the desires of your vehicles (mind, body and emotions), the effect is the same: you hold a belief that somehow you are not equal to isness. You believe that either you are greater or lesser than isness. To respond to the desires of your expressive vehicles with as much passion as you respond to the desires of another's is to honour your equality in isness. You do not need to decide when to put your desires before another's. The vehicles will choose. Sometimes your vehicles will fulfil their desires without regard for another's. Sometimes there will be a joint fulfilment where your desires are being fulfilled at the same time as another's. Then there can be situations where the fulfilment of another's desire comes before your own.

An open heart honours the equality of isness by responding to any desire, whether yours or someone else's, without interference from a closed-hearted self-importance. The heart is 'free' to respond without the constraint of beliefs, ideas, thoughts, feelings, self-preservation, greed or faithlessness. If one continually serves others' desires without serving one's own, greed will result. Greed springs up as a reaction to balance all the giving. A taking must happen to strike a balance with the giving. One who has neglected their own desires eventually reacts by greedily serving themselves to the exclusion of others.

Compassion is the fine balance of serving desires *without regard for their origins.* Selective serving of desires is not compassion. Deciding who to give our attention to and who not to is of the mind. The heart has no decisions to make – it simply responds.

Likewise, serving others' desires with a hope of reward, or serving one's own desires with a sense of guilt, is not compassion. Compassion treads that fine line where servicing of desires is not focused on any individual, but on the service itself. Who is being served or where their desire originated from is of no consequence to compassion. Compassion is the simple, unbiased response of the heart to that with which it interacts. Compassion cannot be tried for – it is free from effort. Anyone trying to give to someone else must inevitably take from them (or a third person) to maintain the sweet balance that isness embodies. Compassion is the tightrope of that balance. To walk it is to concentrate on the balance itself, not on those who are benefiting from the show.

Greed

Greed can exhaust the expressive vehicles. Chasing after unnecessary things is a tiring effort. If we obsessively hold onto 'getting' things, then the expressive vehicles do not have energy to heal themselves with. Their energy is spent on the pursuit of unnecessary and excessive personal gain. The repairs that naturally happen for the survival of the vehicles are interrupted by these demands of greed. The vehicles are used by a greedy heart to pursue benefits for a 'self' or 'person'. They do not therefore have the 'freedom' to get what they need for survival.

A closed heart can become greedy. This greed is a barrier to intimacy. It is an attempt to 'better' isness and thereby break away from it. Isness is like a beautiful gem that can be admired, loved, caressed or valued but *never kept*. Where there is greed, there is always struggle. A greedy heart will always hanker after more in an attempt to 'make things better'. This automatically denies all that is.

Greed can never be satiated. The nature of greed is to *always 'get more'*. Whatever is gained through greed is perceived as 'deserved'. Whatever is not gained through greed is frustrating and 'unfair'. Greed can only end spontaneously. To want greed to end is to try to get something and is greedy.

When the heart is honoured as being open, the individual self no longer exists as a disparate entity. An open heart clearly retains recognition of a self as part of the whole. There is no longer an attempt to gain more power for that self in a non-accepting effort to break away from isness.

Vehicular imbalance

The healthy state for the vehicles is to be in *balance.* This means they are equal in terms of capacity and maturity. When the vehicles are balanced, they can communicate and co-operate as equals and therefore allow for a harmonious and easy life. If one of the vehicles is trained more heavily than the other two then imbalance can result, with the well-trained vehicle becoming domineering over the others.

Vehicular imbalance can be introduced when we are children. Modern scholastic education is often very much geared toward mental development, much less to physical development and almost completely overlooks emotional development. When we have been exposed to such an education system, we have an imbalance in our expressive vehicles. This kind of education trains the mind more than the body and the emotions. The mind then becomes more sophisticated than the other two vehicles. Its expressive capacity is focused heavily in a way that ignores the body and emotions. This kind of education can produce an increased tendency to solve problems with the mind. When this tendency is persisted with, worrying can result. The mind thinks heavily about something even if nothing can be done for it. It indulges in thought processes on a certain topic and the less-developed physical body and emotions may not have a mature enough capacity to express it.

Since our education emphasised mental development, we may also have a conditioned capacity to use intellectual strategies as a protection against direct experience. We can apply these strategies in the form of thoughts and ideas to remove our 'selves' from an experience we have an aversion to. In the example of a sad experience, if sadness is taught as 'wrong', we can escape into the mind in order to temporarily avoid it. The sadness can be thought about instead of being felt, providing a cushion between the experiencer and the experience. Such protection against an experience takes the colour out of life. While it may seem safe to do this, it is actually a closure of the heart and radically reduces our potential to enjoy the richness of life. The enjoyment is in direct experience. Enjoyment and sadness are not necessarily exclusive of each other. Nor are enjoyment and pain, or enjoyment and anger. All can be enjoyed once the shackles of taught aversion spontaneously fall away. Once we cease trying to avoid a certain experience by running away into our mind, we can fully appreciate the diversity that life offers here.

When we stop 'being' our expressive vehicles, we can *be who we are in honour.* Then we can observe our expressive vehicles easily, as if they are at once an integral part of us *and* distant from us. They have the space to *be who they are.* Any imbalances such as an over-developed mind and an under-developed body or emotions, can even out. Once one has surrendered the interference caused by one vehicle controlling another, then the vehicles can manifest their full potential. With no suppression or restraint, they are free to build up the strength they require. They naturally do this for survival. A 'controlling person' puts the survival of their vehicles at risk by trying to change them into a perceived ideal. This is suppression. The only way for the vehicles to be at a peak performance is for them to be free to express as they wish.

Belief

Theories of cause-and-effect are creation myths that explain the 'origins' of the universe. These appear to be self-important human extrapolations. A person takes credit for what they do when they believe that they 'cause' an effect. They see themselves as a 'creator'. Extrapolating this onto a wider scale, the universe is similarly seen as having a 'creator'.

Since our parental influence was an attempt to keep us within moral boundaries, we may reach for a replacement restraint once we grow out of their influence. We may reach for concepts to stand as parental substitutes. Such concepts may include 'god'. 'God' watches over everything, making sure we do the 'right' thing. This projection is a reaching for authority. Believing that an imagined entity or system is watching over us can provide us with a sense of security which can replace the security of parental guidance.

The believer in god often 'separates' himself or herself from *being* by the perception of a 'higher' force. The believer wants this force to 'determine' outcomes based on one's behaviour, just as the parent rewards and punishes. This sense of moral security is an attempt to isolate one's 'self' from the absorbed state that all of us are in. If there is a belief in an entity or system that watches over us and keeps account of our behaviour, then moral rules can become cherished. They seem to be the guidelines that save us from the wrath of a retribution and offer the heaven of a reward.

The belief in causation is born of our humanistic attachment to control. A controller *'causes'* something to happen. They believe that their own power is greater then the rest of isness and therefore believe that they can make things happen. However, the flow of isness moves on whether or not humans believe that they are causing the flow or that the flow is causing them. It makes no difference to the flow how humans perceive it.

Isness is *uncontrollable*. No matter how much seems to be going the way that is wanted, there is no actual control of isness. There is only an appearance of control, and a temporary harmonisation of wants with happenings.

We are the flow. We cannot control the flow. We cannot wholly control ourselves. The perception that we are in control, that the self is choosing everything that happens, is born of our attempts to escape isness. This breakaway from isness cannot happen. The attempt to break away creates a self-importance that makes one feel isolated. Such a separation from isness is impossible.

Power

The appearance of an ability to 'control' happenings can lead one into an experience of power. The belief in one's own self-importance fuels the appearance of 'the power to control'. This 'power' is bound to result in frustration as the 'powerful person' repeatedly watches the very happening that they believe they are in control of go out of control. This is interspersed with the controlling efforts synchronising with a happening that reflects that person's intentions. Here lies pride. Pride is the claim that something happened *because* of one's 'controlling power'.

The power in isness is simple. It is equally spread. No one is more powerful than anyone else. Anyone exerting so-called 'power' over others needs those others to sustain the appearance of being 'more powerful'. The others are equally as powerful as the one claiming 'power' simply because, without them, the claimant's power is no more.

The equal spread of power extends everywhere. Any opinion placing humans in a 'more powerful' position is a denial of isness based on exaggerated self-importance. The root of this self-importance is greed. It is the temptation to try to get more than what is. Underlying all self-importance is the recognition that without greed, the appearance of being 'more powerful' than something else would disappear.

The fear of going out of control keeps most of us from allowing such a recognition. Yet we only have to stop being involved in 'doing' things to see that everything continues *with or without* us. To honour this state of no-control is to effortlessly let emotions and actions play themselves out.

Not knowing the whole

No matter what claims are made with words and concepts, they serve as expressions. They are flavours and pointers, giving expressions through verbal and conceptual communication. To use any words without insisting on their 'truth' or 'reality' is to accept their unpredictably contradictory nature.

'Truth' or 'reality' is simply all that is. Nothing can escape it. These terms are synonymous with isness yet are frequently used to justify opinions and beliefs by terming certain facets of isness 'unreal', 'untrue', or 'false'. Whatever it is called – 'truth', 'reality' or 'isness' – it cannot be known. To know something is to have a relationship to it. We must be at a distance from something to *know* it. If we merge with something, we *are* it. To attempt to 'know' isness, one must become the knower of it. To do this, the human that seeks knowing attempts to separate themselves from isness in order to establish a relationship with it. This separation is impossible. The attempt to escape isness is merely a dishonour of one's nature as being isness. If we *are* isness, we cannot know it. Since we cannot *not be* isness, knowing it is impossible. Unlike knowing, being has no objectification. When the subject becomes the object, both disappear.

Knowing *parts* of isness through objectification is useful. However, we cannot know the whole of isness at once. If we are honouring our nature as isness, then the need to know evaporates. We no longer need to search for what we are if we are *being what we are* (which we all inherently are) and honouring that. The difference between a struggling search for 'truth', 'reality', or 'isness', and a serene surrender to accepting 'truth', 'reality', or 'isness' as who we are, is a simple honour. This honour is born of a spontaneous recognition and the loss of the effort to be something we are not.

To fail and give up can be indicative of a rise to honour. Failure is often viewed by moral codes as undesirable, yet to fail is to not succeed. Success can encourage an effort whereas failure can induce giving up. Without giving up the struggle, it continues. It is the great effort to be other than *what we are* that must be surrendered before the struggle ceases. This surrender is *spontaneous and uncaused*. Any effort to bring it about perpetuates the struggle.

5 The Cessation of Struggle

With the cessation of struggle comes a simplification of one's life. Life can now be honoured as being inherently simple. The tools that were once used to give life a purpose can be dropped. One no longer has to do anything. The effort to do things disappears and, in its place, response appears. Response is a non-interfering way of interacting with isness. Whereas one attempting to control isness may 'do' things with reason, one who has surrendered the attempt to control isness simply responds without reasoning being the overbearing decider. The one who responds listens to the heart's voice. The heart responds. The heart does not 'do' anything. A person can 'do', a heart simply responds. If we give ourselves up to our heart's response, we 'become' our heart. We are all hearts. To recognize this, and to honour it, is to rest without struggle or effort.

Nothing to be done

If we live within the moral code, and at the same time uncontrollably break it, frustration arises. This frustration ceases when the struggle to stay within the boundaries of the moral code ceases. The cessation of struggle happens spontaneously. It cannot be done, for achievement would be another goal defined by the moral code. It would be seen as 'right' to lose the need to live within a moral code, and that judgement writes a new code. Why the entire moral structure should fall away for one and not for another is part of isness. It simply happens or it does not happen.

If we are naturally drawn to heal our wounds, then we may become healthier. However, any method or doing that has the goal of ending struggle is doomed to failure. Struggling ends with the spontaneous, unaided, uncaused recognition that the struggle was only perpetuated by the fear of losing meaning to life, and that now that fear has gone. No one can do this and no one can give it to anyone else. The spontaneous release from struggle is the dissolution of the capacity to invent problems. It is marked by the renewal of purpose and the renewal of one's meaning of life. There can be the ironic recognition that now the bondage of struggle has disappeared, so too has freedom from that bondage. Only the one who is bound perceives freedom. This belief in bondage makes freedom an attractive option. When freedom is recognized to be the same thing as bondage, the whole effort to get free is seen as a reinforcement of bondage.

The only way to bring about the appearance of separation from isness is by a tremendous effort of denial. When this effort is surrendered, our nature as isness can be recognized and then honoured. However, the cessation of effort cannot be done. Any will to end effort involves further effort. Therefore, if effort is to cease, it is in a spontaneous happening, unconnected to time, experience, geography or circumstance.

The street-sweeper and the monk

The end of struggle is available to anyone. So spontaneous and uncaused is it that no one can predict the circumstances that accompany it. Each cessation of struggle is unique. To experience it and to then plot backwards to establish a 'cause' of it is the first step toward the prescription of a 'path'. A 'spiritual teacher' commonly prescribes the methods or circumstances that they were experiencing when their struggle ceased. If indeed it did, for many claiming to be able to pass on information about the 'spirit' are still actually struggling and use their position to give them a sense of purpose or in an attempt to better isness. A teacher can, however, pass on a spiritual vocabulary, which can describe the aspects of struggle ceasing. In this way, one who has learnt this vocabulary from a teacher, either directly or by way of religion, is able to linguistically describe what is occurring if their struggle ends. One who has no connection to a teacher has an equal chance of struggle ceasing, yet may not possess the language to vocalize what is happening. A street-sweeper is as likely to give up, dissolve into their heart, and honour isness as a monk who is fully trained in a religious doctrine. The monk can talk about it more readily, and it is therefore easier for him to rationally understand what has happened. This may bring about the appearance that following a teacher or religious doctrine can bring about the end of struggle. The street-sweeper might not talk about it so no one can listen to him describing what has happened.

What often occurs, though, is a curiosity towards others who have had similar experiences. This attraction naturally shapes who or what we have interest in, who we socialize with or what we read. Through this curiosity, one who spontaneously experiences the cessation of struggle, and all the changes that go with it, can be attracted to those who have experienced a similar happening. In this way, the street-sweeper may find himself moving towards teachers or religion, not to find answers or revelation, but to understand what is happening, and to gain a vocabulary in order to vocalize this amazing experience. To know that others have experienced a similar spontaneous honouring of isness can give one a sense of companionship and can affirm that this is not at all unnatural in a world where denial is widespread.

Struggles accepted

The end of struggle includes the end of struggling with the struggles of others. This acceptance is coupled with the lack of a need to help. When one is 'free' of struggle, there is no need for the struggles of others to cease. They are accepted and the need for them to end dies.

Even after one's moral code has disintegrated, other people will insist on living in a state 'bound' by morals. This 'bondage' is only appearance yet is taken seriously by them and so creates struggle in their lives. To be with another's struggle when your own has ended is acceptance. And acceptance walks hand in hand with cessation of struggle. It naturally exists alongside it. Non-acceptance is struggle. Acceptance is allowing the flow of isness in its constant state of flux to be *as it is*. Acceptance does not bring about the end of struggle or vice versa. They are simultaneous happenings that carry the same flavour.

To sing your own song, it is not necessary to 'free' the group into honouring uniqueness. Also, singing one's own song does not exclude one from harmonising with the group chant at the same time. There is not necessarily a conflict with the group chant when one sings one's own song. There need not be any compromise of one's own honour of uniqueness. One can sing one's own unique song while at the same time ensuring that it matches the key of the group chant. In this way living from your heart does not involve isolation from the wider community.

Enjoyment can only come with acceptance. If we accept something, we can let it through our hearts, and enjoy it. If there is an unconditional acceptance, it is a welcoming of all that is, including all that could be. Sadness, anger, pain, death, loss, grief, confusion and yearning can all be enjoyed when they are accepted. When sadness is enjoyed as much as happiness, pain as much as pleasure, death as much as birth, loss as much as gain, then life itself, whatever its form, is enjoyable. We can simply relax in it, without the unsuccessful struggle to veer it in the direction of what we consider to be 'positive'. We can be in life and give up worrying about whether its form is appropriate or not. This is not apathy but acceptance. When we enjoy life no matter what comes or goes in it, then worries dissolve. Life is a celebration of existence. If it is enjoyed as such, it needn't be obsessed over, frowned upon or exorcized. A song of enjoyment can flow forth forever from our heart, relaxing us, and imbuing us with the gratitude that makes life a wondrous adventure.

Functions returning home

With such an openness of response – to let all be as it is – the functions that were once used for the gain of the 'self' can now return to their original homes. Judgement, a logical function of the mind, returns to its function as a 'discriminating reference point' within the mind. It is no longer used to 'get' for the benefit of one's 'self', yet continues to perform useful functions in order for the mind, body, and emotions to survive. In this way, we have let judgement go out of control and accepted that it is totally conditioned to respond without our input. It is therefore 'freed up' to function without us demanding anything of it. It becomes more balanced. We do not refer to our judgement as a guide to how to live our lives. It is simply a small piece of our make-up that is referred to when it is needed; for example, we can use judgement in situations that offer a logical challenge, such as exactly when to turn right into a busy road. However, to take such a specific function and apply it to every situation in our life is to get stuck in the mind.

The heart responds to all situations. If we honour the heart's response, then it will sometimes refer us to functions within the expressive vehicles. For example, it can refer us to judgement in the mental vehicle for logical calculation, or to enjoyment in the emotional vehicle for confirmation of appropriateness, or to a body part in the physical vehicle for sensual awareness. The heart, left with no interference from greed, simply runs the show. This is where we 'become' the heart, and recognize that *we were always our hearts* but had denied this when we attempted to become something else.

Other functions simply disappear when we melt into our heart. Like our sense of fairness, which was once derived from a judgemental standpoint, and now has no reference. It dissolves to be replaced by an acceptance of the balance of isness. When the balance within isness is recognized, the perception of fairness is absent. Isness is neither fair nor unfair. Everything simply happens. Fairness insists on a possibility of control. Yet with no control, isness is what happens. There is no chance for a fairer isness, for *what happens happens*. It happens without cause.

Another function that returns to its home in the expressive vehicles is motive. One has no motive when dancing to the song of the heart. Motive returns to the mind, body and feeling, and dwells there as a function for the vehicles' survival.

The vehicles are motivated to express themselves. If they are given 'free rein' to express themselves, then they do this in full capacity. Without restriction, restraint, suppression or control, the vehicles abound with energetic play. First of all they offload any stagnant, stuck material, then proceed to express themselves in a fluid way. Patterns and habits formed by the insistent attempt to control isness fall away. Although such patterns and habits may continue with momentum, they gradually cease if the repressive behaviour that nurtured them no longer exists.

Desires with no struggle

When we honour the ease of life, then there is no urgency toward the fulfilment of mental, physical and emotional desires. Movement of the vehicles continues to be toward the fulfilment of desires, however fulfilment is no longer held to be of ultimate importance. Fulfilment and non-fulfilment hold equal ground.

The frustration associated with the non-fulfilment of a desire is present when a 'person' projects relevance onto the fulfilment of it. With the 'person' dissolved into the heart, this projection is no longer there. The vehicles move toward fulfilment of a desire as a natural, healthy function of survival. This is their conditioning. The vehicles, acting like a river flowing down a hill, flow around any obstacles that they may meet. Any obstacle to this flow results in non-fulfilment. Instead of getting stuck at the obstacle and attempting to move it, the uncontrolled vehicles simply flow around it and onwards. They do not have a sense of importance attached to the fulfilment of a desire. If a desire gets left unfulfilled, the vehicles simply flow on to a movement towards the fulfilment of the next desire to arise.

Whether or not the flow toward fulfilment is obstructed is of no relevance to the expressive vehicles *if there are always desires that do get fulfilled and that is sufficient for survival.* If one desire is not fulfilled, then another one may be, and the efficiency of isness moves straight away to whatever other desire may be there without a non-accepting frustration at non-fulfilment. To be non-accepting of an unfulfilled desire is to load that desire with importance, and makes its fulfilment into a challenge. In this way, we can become obsessive in our attempts to fulfil an unfulfilled desire.

There are two main ways in which this obsession can arise. The first is by having a desire and attaching an importance of non-fulfilment to it by repressing it. The second is by having a desire and attaching an importance of fulfilment to it by urgently trying for fulfilment and not accepting the obstacles that prevent that. Either way, the desire becomes important.

All desires seek fulfilment. To repress them through fear that they may never get fulfilled is an attempt to stunt their influence by denial. This builds an obsessive relationship of importance with the desire. To urgently try to fulfil the desires no matter how difficult the removal of obstacles is, is also an obsessive relationship of importance. To let desires flow without interference is to experience ease. In this case, whatever results, fulfilment or non-fulfilment, is of no concern. The desires are not owned. They arise in the expressive vehicles. To hold on to desires as belonging to our 'selves' is to give them an importance that the expressive vehicles do not recognize.

Desires can be enjoyed. Desire is the movement within the mind, body and feelings that keeps them alive. They thrive through desiring. Desire is their life-force and motivation for survival. To enjoy desires without giving them importance is to savour the delicacy of their energetic motion. The motion alone is enjoyable regardless of result. Where a river runs to does not alter the appreciation of its beauty right here, right now.

Madness

Following the heart can break the moral codes and social rules of our community. The will to control the uncontrollable attempts to prevent rules and codes from being broken by denying the heart its expression. The mind provides the reasoning of 'social decorum' and the heart is denied. A strong will to control keeps guard over the possibility of straying away from accepted modes of behaviour. The community often labels unacceptable behaviour as 'mad', yet it is the constraint of the expression of the heart that creates this madness. It is by disallowing strange modes of behaviour that madness can simmer away under the surface appearance of control. To be obsessively in control is to harbour a madness that can fester and mature for as long as the will to control dominates. When the will to control the uncontrollable crumbles and dissolves, the repressed behaviour can purge itself. If this purging is extreme, as in the case of a particularly dominant and long-reigning will to control, the 'mad' behaviour that ensues may be so overwhelming that it actually sets new patterns of regular lifestyle behaviour. One is then 'stuck' in madness.

Any obsession, whether it is with being mad or with not being mad, creates a mad lifestyle. Obsession with sanity suppresses mad 'episodes', and the madness then seeks expression elsewhere. This slow seeping of madness into the life of one who is trying to keep control manifests as a mad lifestyle. Madness is surrender to the loss of control. It is an extreme glimpse of what it is to let control go. Madness is most likely to arise where there has been an obsessive attempt to control. This attempt violently denies the out-of-control nature of isness. When this pretence can no longer be maintained (often due to exhaustion), then madness ensues.

Whatever is constantly suppressed becomes one's life-style. Madness is an extreme deviation from one's habitual routine. It is a healthy purging of deep-seated anxiety. This is natural. The disgust with which madness is often treated stems from a fear that sporadic outbursts of it will reveal that *one's whole lifestyle is mad.* If we can embrace madness without obsession, it simply purges us of burdensome anxiety. If we suppress the expression of madness then our whole lifestyle can become one of madness.

By allowing ourselves to move into unusual forms of behaviour when the heart responds to such desires, we can avoid a mad lifestyle by occasional short expressions of madness.

Conditioning

For the one honouring isness, actions are accepted as simple responses. Nearly all our actions are *conditioned responses*. The claim that we are so important as to be able to change isness is a denial of our conditioned behaviour. Our conditioning behaves for us. We cannot control this. We can try to suppress conditioning only to find it springing unpredictably up in our faces later on. We can deny it but we cannot control conditioning's influence over our behaviour.

We are conditioned by everything we are exposed to and everything we avoid being exposed to. 'Deconditioning' is impossible. Reconditioning happens all the time, however. If someone is laying claim to 'deconditioning' then they have probably been 'reconditioned' by new conditioning to the extent that they no longer recognize their old conditioning. However, as a feature during our lifetime, conditioning cannot be lost or got rid of.

We can trade old conditioning in for new, but even this trade-off stems from our old conditioning. In this way, every influence upon us adds to our conditioning and cumulatively affects us. Those attempting to 'free' themselves from conditioning are denying that we are all conditioned *always*. We are all free *within* our conditioning. To honour this is to negate the need for freedom *from* conditioning.

When we honour our behaviour as being in the hands of conditioning, we can take our hands off the controls. We can let our behaviour move unrestrained according to all the influences we have ever met with. We can also choose with awareness the influences we associate ourselves with for our reconditioning. When we understand the nature of conditioning, we can move towards influences that will regenerate our conditioning in a way that is healing and supportive of growth. Such choices include the people we mix with, the food we eat, the work we do, and the games we play, but more importantly, it is the *way* we do these things. All these influences change our conditioning and therefore change the experience of personal existence. When new conditioning heals, supports, and encourages us, then we no longer feel so constrained by our conditioning.

If we relinquish obsessive control over our behaviour, our conditioning is free from suppression and can express itself fully. In this state, the conditioning is totally fluid and can change rapidly. Old conditioning is played out and new is absorbed. When we allow conditioning to reign over our behaviour without limitations, the conditioning rapidly expresses itself, dies out, and renews itself from a fresh source. The more our conditioning expresses itself without restraint, the less we are influenced by past experiences. The past does not have a stronghold and we can have a renewed feeling of living *here*. Past events can be forgotten as irrelevant, or have the appearance that they happened to someone else. The 'continuity' that is held together by strong past influences falls away and the nature of our lives as perpetually transforming is revealed.

Such a letting go of control must be a sincere release from the heart. It is not an excuse to be irresponsible or malicious, but rather a way to give up the unnecessary burden of constant moral enforcement. One who does not use moral policing to control their behaviour will gradually witness the death of old conditioning, and the birth of new, at a faster rate than when a moral code was in effect. This speeding up of conditioning's regeneration can give the feeling that time is expanding. So much transformation appears to happen that it is as if time has enlarged itself. The changes one might have experienced in a month may now happen in a day. This process is directly relative to our acceptance of isness. If we accept that every part within isness is continually changing, then this is our experience. If we do this we experience 'slow change'. When we fall into acceptance, and out of denial, our experience can be one of 'change occurring more frequently'.

Responders of the heart

If one of the three expressive vehicles (the mind, the emotions or the physical body) has been obsessively used as a reference for "what to do" and "how to do it", then a spontaneous opening of the heart can bring about a balancing scenario.

Obsessive attachment to an expressive vehicle as a guide commonly takes the form of reference to moral values in the mind, however it can also be one of continual emotional or physical reference. Whichever vehicle is referred to, the process is the same – the vehicle is consulted as a guide for decision-making or to affirm the 'correct' action in a situation. When and if one spontaneously gives up this effort of reference, the heart can shine forth, and be followed instead. When this happens, the heart moves, and the vehicles follow. Then the heart is the only guide. The vehicles become mere 'responders of the heart' instead of acting as guides. They feed back information to the heart, the heart gives direction to the vehicles, and in turn the vehicles respond to this direction.

With a continual honouring of the heart, the heart appears to open and melt outwards, absorbing the vehicles. This crumbling of resistance in the heart gives the appearance of a 'growth of heart'.

When the vehicles are absorbed in the heart, or when their inherent absorbed-in-the-heart state is recognized and honoured, the vehicles and the heart flow as one. There is no more effort to separate them. They were never separate from each other, yet the constant reference to the vehicles whilst the heart was ignored gave the appearance that they were not joined together. The vehicles return to their roles as *expressions of the heart*. Reference to anything, the vehicles *or* the heart, becomes meaningless. Since they are one and the same, any expression in a vehicle is a direct response *of* the heart.

There is an interim balancing stage where the vehicles are recognized as a direct response *to* the heart. Once this happens, we can recognize that *we are our heart*, and can let life live itself out through sheer response. It is then that the vehicles are responders *of* the heart.

Authenticity is rooted in the initial honouring and following of the heart. This way of life totally overrides the need for control. To be authentic is to let all vehicles go uncontrolled. To be authentic is to give up controlling the vehicles even when to do so could create unexpected results. This is allowed even if it appears that we risk losing something 'valuable', or if we begin to move in ways that are outside of social habit. To be authentic is to honour who you are without restraint and without concern for the consequences. With awareness of the innate connection between heart and vehicles, every action is recognized as an absorbed expression of love.

Once the vehicles are released from any attempts to better isness then space opens up between them. The space manifests as unmixed desiring. In vehicles that are not 'controlled', each vehicle desires *for itself*. With a balanced reign between the vehicles, each vehicle rules for itself, yet is fully integrated with the other two vehicles by means of communication. Each vehicle reclaims autonomy in terms of its own essential behaviour, yet continues to describe this behaviour to the other two vehicles. In this state, the mind becomes a reference point to describe in thoughts and ideas what is appropriate and healthy behaviour for the emotions and body. The input that forms these thoughts comes directly from the emotions or from the body, unlike thoughts based on a moral code that come from external mental perceptions. To put it simply, if the mind relaxes and gives up the attempt to control the emotions, the body, and itself by applying morals, then the voice of each vehicle can clearly be heard. These voices let each vehicle know what is healthy and appropriate for it. The body tells the body, the feelings tell the feelings, and the mind tells the mind. In this instance, the mix-up between vehicles is resolved. One manifestation of this resolution could be the end of inappropriate sovereignty. For example, sex that may have been sought after for emotional reasons can now be sought after for sexual reasons. Eating that was decided on by the mind can be decided on by the body. Thoughts that were provoked by the body can instead be derived from the mind. In this way, there is *space* in the vehicular system.

In this scenario, each vehicle chooses for itself while communicating to the other two vehicles about the decisions made. The vehicles are not separate but because they have space they can co-operate more efficiently. This can also be seen in human relationships, where two people choose for themselves while openly communicating to each other about those choices. A certain amount of space between them can allow each person a more fulfilling independence as well as the joy of intimate communication.

The communication between vehicles takes the form of a signal from one vehicle manifesting in another. For example, if the body requires food, the signal of hunger can manifest in the mind. A thought can then affirm that the body is hungry, yet this is vastly different to the mind deciding wholesale that the body should eat. It is simply an echo of the body's voice in the mind, not the mind commanding the body.

One can absolutely honour the heart by giving all vehicles a 'free rein' in expression. The vehicles decline to interfere with one another, instead concentrating their energies *within themselves*. This strengthens the mind, the emotions and the body. Without territorial invasion happening between the vehicles, they are able to function independently and in harmony with each other. The honouring of the ease of life produces a wondrous vehicle: a meld of mind, feelings, and matter, which emanates a distinct energy, one of comparative strength.

In the physical body, this can manifest as a natural ease in relation to eating, sex and fitness. A body that is not being 'controlled' or restrained has a maximum chance of fulfilling its desires. One who is struggling to 'stay in control' pushes an authoritarian restraint on the body. The body is used to 'get' something in an attempt to hold together the appearance that one is coping and 'in control'. If the effort to control the body spontaneously ceases, then the body is 'free' to follow its own desires and not those of a greedy person.

Left to follow their own desires, the vehicles do so without being greedy. Greed is an attempt to get something more than is necessary. When a body is not polluted by an effort to obsessively control it, it will simply follow desires that are programmed in it for its own survival and for that of the human species. Breathing, drinking and eating are the functions that the human body survives by. If these are catered for, then sex can perpetuate the survival of the human species. Usually, the body desires these functions in varying strengths, breathing being the strongest, followed by drinking, then eating, and lastly sex. These desires, and their varying strengths, are easily seen if the body is deprived of any of them. The body can only survive a short time without air, a longer time without water, even longer without food, and a very long time without sex. The species, for its survival, relies on human bodies fulfilling their desires for the first three fundamentals followed then by sex.

A body that is given 'freedom' to roam in search of fulfil-ment of its desires is getting what it needs to survive when it needs it. In this way, a body that is 'free' can heal itself, feed itself and maintain itself with maximum efficiency. If a person supports the mental projection of moral judgments that constrain the body, this detracts from the efficiency of a body. In short, a 'free' body will eat and drink well (even if it contradicts learnt ideas of what 'well' is), will get fit (even if the methods it uses to do so are unusual), will breathe as best suits it (without emotional interference), and will move into sexual encounters for the propagation of itself and the species (whether or not the encounters adhere to social 'norms'). These actions are ruled by *ease*. If an action can fulfil a desire easily, it is made. If it is not easy, it is not made. For example, if an action risks damage to a vehicle or to the species, then the body will decline and leave the desire unfulfilled forever. An unfulfilled desire will not surface as a repressed desire later on if it has been followed all the way to the point where the movement toward fulfilment stopped being easy. The need to fulfil a desire disappears when the body is convinced that it is not easy to fulfil. Like a river meeting a rock, the body moves around an obstruction to its desire. It does not wait there insisting that the obstruction move out of its way. In this way, the body has no care for fulfilment of desires yet pursues them up to the point where it is no longer easy.

Vehicular blow-out

To 'sing your own song' is to let the heart sing unrestrained. To dance to the song of the heart is to follow it without concern for how that manifests in the material, emotional and mental planes. To let the restraining influence of boundaries collapse is to honour our nature as being unbounded. This vast letting-in can unleash previously repressed energy from the heart. Energy that sought expression in the physical, mental and emotional vehicles, but that was deterred through moral control, has an opportunity to complete its desired expression once there is no moral reference. An honouring of the out-of-control nature of isness can allow this stifled energy to come out. Furthermore, the physical body, the emotions and the mind through which it is expressed are not used to embodying so much force. They are 'out of training'. In this way, if the restraints of moral conduct dissolve, and one dances to the song of the heart, there may be some initial shock.

Where there is uncontrolled energy rising from the heart and manifesting in the expression that is most appropriate to the energy (not to a moral code), then the expressive vehicles are well exercised in embodying this flow. Children can be like this. The application of a moral code attempts to stifle this flow. If energy seeks expression somewhere that is 'wrong', the moral code says that it must be prevented. The applied code either channels the expression towards somewhere 'right', or totally prevents it, in which case it is suppressed and lies latent. If, after some time, the moral code disintegrates, this channelling can no longer be implemented. Energy is then 'freed' to express itself wherever it is drawn to as being most appropriate. Unrestrained, it moves wherever it 'chooses'. Such an energetic uprising is merely the effect of no longer suppressing our naturally open hearts. The effort to force the heart closed through moral policing is not there, and there can be a return to the unlimited heart-flow that we experienced in our first years of life.

The combination of a renewed honouring of uncontrollability that lets energy move anywhere, the unleashing of a backlog of repressed energy, and the expressive vehicles' lack of practice at embodying excessive energy, can lead to vehicular blow-out. The mind, body and emotions can be blown apart, resulting in excessive strain. The vehicles matured during a period where morals restricted their expression. When the heart opens, and there is no longer moral constraint on their expressive form, then the impact of the flow upon the vehicles may be greater than they are prepared for. This can lead to breakdown in these vehicles simply because the force of flow through them was too great. The result can be both a new temporary damage and an awareness of old damage. At first, this can be painful, yet if responded to (and with a free-flowing energy from the heart, response is all there is), then they can adjust to 're-train' and strengthen to accommodate the new flow. It is akin to an athlete whose passion is to run, yet through moral judgements stops himself from doing so. The physique deteriorates. Then, one day, the moral judgements cease. Overjoyed, the athlete goes running. He is grateful that he can run and is bewildered as to why there was ever a decision to suppress his passion. And although it feels so natural and healthy to be running, the physique of the athlete is not up to it, and pain is felt as the body readjusts and strengthens to the new honouring of passion.

When the vehicles readjust to the wave of newness that an openly expressive heart brings, then they can experience a heightened vitality that can take them to new strengths. When the vehicles recover from their initial blow-out, they can rebuild in a way that encompasses the unlimited energetic flow that has been rediscovered. In this way, although the initial effects of moral code disintegration may be traumatic for the vehicles, they can eventually become much more toned in strength than ever before.

Vehicular blow-outs may appear to be traumatic, yet the violent force with which they occur is only relative to the force that constrained the energy in the first place. To judge anything as 'right' or 'wrong' and then make 'controlled decisions' based on that is to use force. It is a force that will 'spring back in one's face'. It will react by coming back with as much force as was used to push it down.

The mind, body, and emotions all have needs and desires which draw them toward certain things. A greedy heart will claim a 'person' out of these expressive vehicles by combining them together and using them to get something that is not needed. At its root, greed is the attempt to 'better' isness. Only when the attempt has irreversibly failed will greed come to an end. To 'better' isness is impossible. To recognize the impossibility of 'bettering' isness is to give up.

Once the struggle to better isness ceases, then the control that is exercised over the vehicles to this end also ceases. The expressive vehicles continue to have needs. The difference is that without greed they are unconstrained by a 'person' and are 'free' to roam in search of the object of their need. A need of an expressive vehicle is born of the will to survive. Such a need is for the functioning of the vehicle. Expressive vehicles unrestrained by greed or moral judgements have optimum potential for survival. An expressive vehicle moving toward something for its survival is an absorbed expression of isness.

Healing

The recognition of our innate qualities brings about a clarity of that which may be called 'spirit'. Once we have looked deeply and remembered who we are, that same clarity can be turned outward into the expressive vehicles. When we are honouring our nature with conscious love, we can see all aspects of our vehicles. The aspects we most commonly avoid in them are our diseases. These may have been too frightening to look at, so we pushed them away and did not accept this 'dark side' within us. Those aspects of our vehicles that are functional, healthy and pleasure-giving are more readily accepted. The mental, emotional and physical diseases, however, are often the last to be acknowledged. When we carry the flavour of our inner spirit into the expressive vehicles, then they can be healed.

We can see the disease, and we can see the pathways to healing. This is so grounding. Through healing, our vehicles begin to harmonize with the spirit by reflecting the qualities of it. Healed vehicles can carry our spirit in a way that resonates fully with who we are as a whole. These aspects of our vehicles that we once pushed away can again be reunited.

When we accept our 'dark side' we can honour our nature as whole. Without the effort to deny an aspect of our vehicles, our innate wholeness is beheld, respected and then acted upon in the vehicles. We can once again experience the vehicles as a holistic grounding point for the spirit. With wholeness in the vehicles, they have the capacity to fully express spirit. They grow to encompass the flow of expression that continually passes through them. In this way, healing is maturing. Mature vehicles are whole vehicles. We are our vehicles as well as our spirit, and therefore any denial on either side means missing the maturing process that allows the dance of life to be vibrantly celebrated.

While looking inward, our innate qualities may be revealed. With this recognition, looking outward can heal our vehicles. To do one while denying the other is to lose a wondrous and potentially enjoyable part of our existence. A natural balance between all facets of who we are gives us maximum potential for joy.

Grounding

When we look inward, we can experience the recognition that our heart is spirit. To sing one's own song is to allow what we are as spirit to make unobstructed contact with our vehicles.

When we allow spirit to flow into form we become aware of the blockages within the vehicles that are preventing a full flow. To sing one's own song with courage and without shame is to expose these blocks and to allow them to dissolve. If blocks exist in our vehicles, then spirit does not appear to flow fully into form. It always does, however, because the nature of spirit and form are identical – they are one and the same. Vehicular blocks give the *appearance* of separation between spirit and form because spirit flows into the blocks and manifests there. This means that spirit does not flow into vehicular expression, and is therefore not manifesting in a tangible, creative way. When we feel low on energy, this is because the flow of spirit is restricted to our vehicular blockages and is not readily available in expression. In this state, it appears as though spirit needs a contact point in matter. It appears as though spirit is not flowing into form. For the sake of wholeness, spirit needs a worldly grounding point. Disease in the vehicles seems to prevent us from living to our full potential as wholeness.

If spirit is allowed a full, unobstructed flow into form, then the separation between sprit and matter is no longer perceived. All is seen as one. Everything is recognized as spiritual. When we deny this due to the lack of awareness of our nature as spirit, then we reach for wholeness in our vehicles. This is why the group chant is so attractive. The hope is that wholeness can be achieved by doing the same as everyone else. The hope is that by following the group chant of society's values, then we can *do* the same as other humans, thereby getting as close as we can to *being* the same as them.

However, if we recognize spirit as an inherent aspect of who we are, then we can clearly see that we are all one. This recognition can release our effort to realize this through the group chant, and can lead to an honouring of our uniqueness in form.

As spirit, we are all one and the same. As vehicles, we are distinctly different. When we honour our unity as spirit and our diversity as vehicular forms, then we can sing our own song without forgetting our essential nature. Spirit can then flow forth in our vehicles as a vibrant manifestation. This is our heart in action.

The more the vehicular blocks vanish, the more this flow opens up. If tension is held in the body, or emotions are left suppressed, then spirit gets into this tension, and cannot therefore flow into a creative expressive form. In this way, vehicular tensions prevent us from living to our full individual potential as a manifestation of spirit. An overactive mind can also interfere in this process. If we think about our lives so much that it takes our focus away from our awareness of who we are, then we forget our spirit aspect and get caught in the group chant as a hope for wholeness.

It is only when we can allow spirit to make full contact in the world that we sing our own song clearly and expressively. The form of the contact point that we consciously allow spirit to flow into can be beyond prediction and may only be understood after it has happened. When we allow spirit to flow fully into form, and we allow the fear of how it might manifest to be felt but not to be restrictive, then we can recognize that spirit and form are one and the same. The belief in separation stems from the vehicular blocks that stunt the flow of spirit into expression. The more spirit flows into blocks, the less it can manifest as one's song.

To let all be as it is, is to appreciate our flow into form, no matter how restricted this is by blocks. Spirit and world are one, regardless of how we perceive it. Our perception can align with this inherent feature more easily once our vehicles are actively representing spirit. This active representation can happen when the vehicles no longer restrict spirit's expressive flow either by being tense or by focusing on themselves at the cost of forgetting spirit as an aspect.

The inward-looking that brings the recognition of who we are as spirit must be balanced by the outward-looking that brings us the recognition of who we are as worldly humans. When there is a balance and maturity in recognizing our inner and outer aspects, then inner and outer are known to be the same, and are no longer two distinct aspects of us. This is wholeness. Singing one's own song is a unique and diverse celebration of this wholeness.

Gratitude

A common response in the honouring of isness is gratitude. Gratitude is the melting heart's response to the glory of being honourable to isness. Gratitude is a sweet 'thank you' for the resting that *being love* is. Gratitude manifests emotionally as a loving response to the experience of being immersed in love.

Isness is love. 'Love' is commonly used to describe relationships yet love is an absolute that permeates the whole of isness. Love is the flavour of isness. To honour isness is to recognize the essence of it, and therefore who we are, as love.

Gratitude brings this recognition into the world of form. To experience gratitude is to be moved effortlessly to a sharing. Gratitude is the thankfulness of unity. It is the overwhelming sense that one is fortunate to be relieved from the burdens of effort, denial and struggle. This gratitude manifests physically as an increase in body energy. It moves into action as a spontaneous sharing. It is a response to the relief of recognising our unbound nature mixed with a wish to share that with others.

There is no motive in the responsive action that stems from gratitude. Gratitude is simply the feeling that one has been given to, and the natural movement to this is to give back. Although nothing has been gained and nothing can be given, the feeling of gratitude nonetheless propels one into sharing. Each human has talents that were shaped by their conditioning. One of the manifestations of a grateful response is to share those talents with the world, solely for enjoyment, both one's own and others'.

6 *Isness*

Isness can be described as 'that which is'. It encompasses everything and nothing. It includes 'spiritual' and 'material'. It is immediate. There is nothing outside of it. We are isness. If we perceive ourselves beyond this it is merely conceptual conjecture. Isness needs no concept. It is 'what is'. Anything further to this is also a part of 'what is'. Any perception or concept cannot directly tell us who we are. We are who we are. The deepest description of isness is beyond language. It is a direct response that accepts isness *as it is*. It is devoid of thought, feeling, matter, mysticism, time, or place, yet it is not disturbed by any of these.

To define isness is impossible. Whatever is said is contradictory to it. Words are fragmentary and cannot therefore encompass the entirety of isness, although every word still carries the flavour of it. When isness is being described, it is a seemingly impossible contradiction that continues until words collapse into a direct experience.

Language

Some words have been given special status and importance. In the cloaked world of human 'mysticism', there is often a reliance on the belief that there is a state or a type of being that can be attained. This makes the 'one who has attained' seem important. The term 'god' has been given personal qualities as 'one who certain humans may be in contact with and others not'. The word 'consciousness' has been used in terms of 'higher' and 'lower' to designate rankings in human hierarchies.

If we move our expression in line with the simplicity of the heart, our language will follow. The beauty of words is in how absent a 'person' is when they are formed. With no 'person' present, the heart flows into language with a simplicity that is not motivated by self-importance. With no 'self' being held together, our expressions are free to run wild from the heart.

Isness is divine. We do not need to formulate concepts to recognize the divinity in everything. Concepts merely describe it. Isness is at once who we are, the experience of who we are as a part of that, and the experience of everything else as a part of that. This is where logic fails. We are isness. We are all that is. At the same time, we are one part of the whole, and can experience and interact with all the other parts. The mind's rational thought calculates an 'either/or' scenario. However, direct experience can blow away any intellectual speculation to show that we are simultaneously all that is *and* a part of it. This is who the 'I' is.

You are neither exclusively spirit nor matter. You are both. Any bias towards one suggests a previous bias towards the other. You exist everywhere and you exist in one heart, one mind, one body, and one group of feelings. Just because rational thinking cannot understand this does not mean it cannot be experienced. Every seemingly separate aspect of life is inherently one. The unity is in the sharing: every fragment is part of isness. Recognising this, boundaries become games, not limitations. This recognition can spark anywhere and is not dependent on who you are, what you do, or how you behave. We all experience our selves as fragments, yet if we take that to be all we are, then a sense of isolation can ensue. Refuge from this isolation can be sought by reaching for others or trying to change our environment, but ultimately without success. The only way we can have a sustained experience of wholeness is by recognising our unity as well as our fragmentary nature. People are fragments. Recognition of our essential wholeness is simply the fragment looking inside deeply enough towards the whole so that there is no doubt of its inherent unity. A fragment that has recognized this can be content as a fragment. To see one's wholeness in doubtless clarity is to rest contented in the apparent paradox of being the whole and a fragment simultaneously.

In the open experience of isness, one is completely melded with the entire cosmos and yet able to function in a thinking, feeling, flesh-suit in a remote part of that cosmos. To function in an experience of the inherent unity of all that is, is to fall open at the heart and flow from it in ease, enjoyment, love and sharing.

Acceptance

Acceptance is something we are all very familiar with. When we were young, we accepted isness. The subsequent loss of acceptance can only be regained when we accept *ourselves*. This is the greatest hurdle. To accept oneself as being who one is can appear difficult because the effort to separate our 'self' from isness has been so great. We know what we have done, but often cannot admit it. To be honest about our efforts to isolate our 'selves' from isness is to see our own greed. This can lead to a self-hatred, and a wish to get rid of the 'self'. Acceptance of the 'self' is a first major step into the acceptance of isness.

When we are in self-acceptance, it becomes clear that all others do not share the same space. It is also clear that all others do not accept *us*. The next step after self-acceptance is the acceptance of those close to us, who live or have lived around us. Whenever we come to acceptance, it is always preceded by emotional purging. To accept is to be clear emotionally. With jammed emotions, reactions prevent acceptance. Emotions like anger and sadness must be expressed before acceptance can happen. Falling into acceptance is to let emotional uprising express itself in the way *it* chooses. The more we try to suppress emotional expression, the more it remains stagnant within us. Giving an emotion the respect and the space it needs to express itself will allow it to clear itself out.

The hallmarks of self-acceptance are honesty and a capacity to be who you are whatever the circumstances. If we defend our 'selves' against life's experiences to the point of isolation, then we are in fear and deny the equal nature of isness. Acceptance and denial are mutually exclusive. In acceptance, we can only honour isness. Any denial in an attempt to make isness 'better', demolishes acceptance. Acceptance is the ultimate rest. Everything is let be as it is, without an urgent need for it to either change or stay still. Acceptance cannot be done. Acceptance is a death of cling-ing to 'heaven', and the 'right ways to be'. Death happens. It cannot be done. With anything that is done making no dif-ference to acceptance, one can relax and explore enjoyment.

Happiness is a wondrous experience, and if sadness is honoured as equally wondrous, neither 'ups' nor 'downs' lose their awesome capacity for enjoyment. Then there is no longer a searching for 'highs' or discontentment with 'lows'. All is as it is. The judgement of what is 'good' and what is 'bad' remains a function of the mind. The difference is that judgement is no longer used by the heart as a reference point for how to behave, how to flow, how to be or what to be. The heart is 'freed up' from continually having to examine an intellectual moral before expression. This 'freedom' is always there and could be spontaneously available to anyone, anytime. However, it is often the case that it is blocked by a non-acceptance deriving from an involvement in the moral code. When isness is accepted it has homeliness about it. With acceptance, there is no more struggle, no more fighting with isness. There is a sharing, and it is one of *being isness*. For if we accept our 'selves', then accept 'others', and finally accept isness, we find that we are isness, and always were. It is just that now we can stop denying it, and instead honour it with acceptance and gratitude.

The absorbed 'I'

To rest in the void is to dissolve the 'I' (or the 'self') into isness in acceptance. With no moral reference, no parent, teacher, or doctrine, there is no guidance as to the 'correct' way of being or doing. 'I' no longer refers to an 'outside' source for assistance. 'I' honours its nature as isness and heals the division between 'I' and 'authority'. 'I' honours its dissolution in isness and becomes the authority that was once sought for 'outside' of 'I'. This is a resting in the void. This is a falling without direction from the dishonour of an isolated 'I' into the honour of an 'I' absorbed in isness. There is no reason for resting in the void, and no choice. Those who have unified a once isolated 'I' and begin honouring isness do not *do* this. It simply happens.

An absorption *in* isness naturally leads to an awareness of isness. When we honour our nature *as isness*, we can simply see *what is*. The absorption of 'I' into isness comes with a mixture of relief and grief. At last one can honour isness and live life without denial. At the same time, the one who has denied has been lost. The one who denies their nature insists that they are separate from isness. When absorption of the 'I' into isness occurs, there is nowhere left to go. There is acceptance of nothing being outside of isness. Therefore anything previously attempting this must die.

We *are* isness. To honour our nature as totally absorbed in isness is to be unique. Isness is unique. Isness is uninfluenced. Every part of isness is influenced by every other part, but isness itself does not stand alone or separate from anything. All is isness, and there is nothing outside of it to influence it. It is therefore totally unique without comparison with anything else.

To be absorbed in isness is to be open to all that is. We are isness, therefore we cannot shut any of isness out. Any attempt to do this is dishonourable and does not succeed anyhow. If there is an honour of our inherent nature as isness, then there is no attempt to break away from it. An acceptance of being isness coincides with the end of struggle. Life is then honoured as it is – essentially easy. All difficulty is invented. When the invention of difficulty ceases, so does difficulty itself. 'Easy' simply means that no effort is required to be who we are. It means that struggle is no longer a part of life, much less the focus of it.

Renunciation of difficulties is of little help. Wherever there is renunciation, there is a motive to renounce. If the motive to renounce carries an attempt to 'better' isness then it is dishonourable. 'Bettering' isness is impossible. Anything considered 'better' than isness is isness. It simply cannot be bettered. This is the nature of isness. It is all that is.

Opening out into absorption

The opening out into the vulnerability of absorption can be seen to happen in four stages. First, there is a loss of personal power. This is the most painful stage. This is the only stage where there is anything to lose. What is lost is the ownership of everything that was once owned. Nothing is 'yours' anymore. Nothing is deserved or coveted by a 'right' to it. Only when nothing is owned can we cease to keep things, letting all be as it is without effort. Only when we let everything be without obsessive ownership can we appreciate the delightful gift of isness.

The second stage is falling into the lap of the universe. Isness cradles us and everything is taken care of. All happens as if it were perfect. Synchronicities are abundant, and even the unknown has a hint of familiarity. This is always how it is, yet in opening out into absorption, we are allowing ourselves to see this in the nurturing omnipotence of isness. We have surrendered to isness and can therefore recognize its eternal characteristics.

In the third stage, the self seems to become the universe. In fact, the self *always is* the entire universe. Yet, only a wide-open heart can recognize that without fear. It is fear that prompts a closing of the heart and the subsequent appearance of separation from isness. An open heart is effortless. To be open-hearted is simply to honour what is. Nothing need be done. Actions make no difference to the heart. Denial closes it, honour opens it, and we have no choice as to which happens. Honour is a spontaneous happening. An open heart spontaneously blossoms like a flower in its ripeness, and grows to consume the separation that it once tried to maintain. With no separation, or fear, and with openness, honesty, acceptance, and honour, we are isness, we know who we are, and we celebrate it. Isness is a celebration of being itself.

The fourth stage is a renewal of personal power. With the self being experienced as isness, this power can flow into one's life without attachment. It is as though, having been stripped of everything, you are now gifted with it all back again, but this time you have no obsession with it and can therefore use it and play with it in a much more powerful way. One who has recognized their essential unified nature can grow anew their personal power without greed, abuse or fear. They can roll through life, enjoying their new sense of health and energy. These people can bring a beautiful creative contribution to the world through acts of joyful compassion.

When personal power is connected via the heart to the spirit without the obstruction of fear, then it can grow beyond any previous experience of it. To remove such obstructions is to face your fear. The spontaneous recognition of your essential nature can give you the capacity to face your fears head-on, and to live through them so that they may melt. The four stages of losing personal power, dancing with isness, becoming isness and finally reclaiming your personal uniqueness with increased power, allow one to open out into absorption and be one without fear.

Causality

Whether or not a cause of isness exists when one cannot be seen is irrelevant. Isness is all that is. The need for there to be a cause of isness, or for isness to be an effect, is an attempt to reinforce one's own status as a cause. If we give up our stance of exaggerated personal importance, then the absorption of 'I' into isness clearly displays that we simply *are*. We did not cause any of isness, and we were not caused by any of it. We are inextricably linked to all that is. Isness is a network. The hierarchical perception of isness is based on the belief that power is distributed throughout isness in unequal amounts. The belief of being more powerful or less powerful than anything else creates this hierarchical viewpoint. The self-important human holds onto the idea that some 'more powerful' force must be the 'cause' of isness. This belief requires a sustained perception of a 'self' that is isolated from isness. If we honour our nature as being isness, then the belief in a more or less powerful force is a mere function of the mind, and is not something on which to base the bigger picture of 'what it is to exist and how to behave within this existence'.

The mind has no part to play in the way that power is balanced throughout isness. Yet, with a perceived power hierarchy, the mind has the opportunity to create fantastic reasons for the existence of isness that are then followed in one's lifestyle. Creators, causes and stories are all invented to reassure the self-important human that somehow they are 'detached' or 'separate' from the whole. This kind of exaggerated personal importance is perpetuated by the fear of personal death. When the 'I' is absorbed into isness as a part of it, then a hierarchical view of the universe can be given up.

Time

The perception of time gives us past, present and future. Through this perception, isness is seen as a series of events happening sequentially, one after the other. When we drop perception of all kind and cease to use a learnt value system to view isness through, then a collapse of 'I' into isness can occur. This is where 'I' surrenders to isness and becomes subsumed by it, immersed and swimming in it. Taking nothing and with no purpose, 'I' and isness unify. 'I' can then report on isness.

Isness does not happen sequentially. There is no event timing. Those events that can be perceived as occurring in time are occurring simultaneously with no time. Every happening is happening all the time. When 'I' is immersed in isness, time becomes redundant as a tool to measure the universe by. It remains useful as a means to synchronize with other humans and to make predictions based on past experience, yet its limitations render it useless for recognising the nature of isness. For example, we perceive a tree to have leaves in summer and none in winter. This appears to be two distinct and different states. In the transition between having leaves and losing them, we perceive time. The simultaneous nature of isness is that the tree has leaves *and* has no leaves simultaneously, and eternally. The perception of time comes from our experience of different aspects of this singular phenomenon. We experience the tree with leaves and then we experience it with no leaves. We also experience all the stages in between. When we link all these experiences together in the perceptive mechanisms of the mind, we say time has occurred. What has occurred, though, is a movement of experience through the different states of the tree. We project this travelling outward and perceive the 'outside' world to be changing.

'I' is change. The intimacy of 'I' with events means that 'I' is the ever-changing events surrounding the body and mind. 'I' always changes. Awareness of 'I' remains constant, unless 'I' is dissolved in isness. When 'I' is dissolved in isness, awareness of isness prevails. Since 'I' is always inherently melted with isness, it is only the shift of awareness from the limited 'I' to the unlimited isness that occurs.

Stillness

There is a balance in nature. It is a stillness based on an equality of changes. All parts of the universe are constantly changing, and this in itself is stillness. The forms of these changes are infinite and are therefore beyond analysis of the mind. The mind functions through limitation and cannot understand infinity, although at the pinnacle of thought it can surrender to the vastness of it. Any concept that is invented to explain the stable balance of changes is unable to reveal the form that this will take. If a balance is simply seen without an attempt to understand the form of it, then the 'right' way to live does not exist and the construction of moral guidelines is not necessary.

Isness is a stable equality of instabilities. Isness as a whole is the only one that essentially does not change. The whole cannot be any other. Whatever parts are taken or added to a whole, it remains a whole. While the parts of the whole are constantly changing, the essence of whole remains unchanged. It is always 'all that is'.

To attempt to keep still the changing parts of isness is an unconscious search to recognize isness in its entirety. The only stillness is isness. To try to bring stillness about in any part of isness is futile. The nature of that which is within isness is constant change. To try to change something that is always changing is unnecessarily tiring. It is an attempt to change things in a way that is 'best' or preferable. This does not succeed. Even if the flow of isness mirrors one's intentions to 'control' it, inevitably the flow will again move in a direction that is not 'best' or preferred. The attempt to control the flow of isness detracts from the enjoyment of it. Even when the flow goes the way that is 'best', it cannot be enjoyed for fear of losing it. If we do not try to change what is, we can enjoy the continual change that always goes on within isness.

To try to change the flow of isness is an asking for stability. Attempts to control are, at their core, a wish for stability. The thoughts may be 'If only something would stay', or 'If only I could keep something and not lose it'. The attempt to keep something is a denial of the transitory nature within isness. Everything is always changing. The only non-transitory one is isness itself, in its entirety. The parts change while the whole remains.

There is only one whole. The search to return to this one can begin with the attempt to 'realize' it within the parts. The underlying motive is often, 'If only I could just stop a part from changing, I would recognize the whole'. This effort is futile and frustrating. Like running water, whatever is held onto slips away. Whatever you try to keep, you lose. We can only lose something we are, or have been, holding onto. To deny this is to perpetually try to 'make up' for lost things by holding onto new ones. It is only when the transitory flow of isness is recognized and honoured, that we can release our grip. Then we can see that no matter how hard we try to pin something down, it will change. In this acceptance, we can recognize the one that is changeless, the essential nature of isness as a whole.

7 *Emotions*

Emotions are mechanisms for the survival of mind and body. They mark boundaries by rising up. To allow this uprising and to respect those boundaries is to operate within them for physical and mental survival. Illness of both mind and body can result if the emotional uprising is not given the freedom to mark boundaries. To let the emotions express themselves as and when they wish to is to allow them to set boundaries. These boundaries are essential for mental and physical well-being. Fear, sadness, anger, happiness, and all the other emotions serve to provide a healthy environment in which the mind and body can grow.

Streams

Emotions run in streams within us. Each person encompasses a unique balance of emotional streams. The breadth of each of these emotional streams can change over time. When we feel an emotion, it appears to be caused by a situation. However, a situation can only bring our attention to an emotional stream running within us. These streams manifest physically in our body as gestures, expressions and style as well as forming the way our body looks. The wrinkles on our face, our posture as we stand or sit, and everything else that our body represents have been shaped by emotional streams. One body differs from another according in part to their emotional streams. One body may be heavily weighted by anger, another by sadness.

When a situation brings our focus to one or more emotional streams, we are conscious of them. If we allow their expression, we do not 'dam' the stream in an attempt to prevent its expression. This damming action manifests as tension in the body. Damming an emotional stream only serves to widen its breadth in proportion to all the other streams. Eventually, the dam bursts and in the meantime, the stream's breadth has grown so much that the emotional uprising is overwhelming and its expression cannot be prevented. Such is the extreme release that follows an attempt to inhibit an emotion.

Triggers

When emotion is suppressed it is stored away until it is triggered. A trigger can bring up suppressed emotion. A trigger is any person or situation that puts us in touch with an emotion that has been ignored. They do this by penetrating our defences of avoidance or denial. Triggers can stimulate sluggish, unexpressed emotion and aid in its fluid expression. In a more extreme way, a trigger can facilitate an unleashing of suppressed emotion in the form of an uncontrolled outburst. The one experiencing this outburst can blame the trigger for the intensity of the emotional expression, yet it is the act of suppression that causes a backlog. The trigger merely sets it off. The trigger initiates the clearing of emotional backlog. When triggered, the emotional backlog (or part of it) comes out. In this way, the triggering of suppressed emotion causes emotional displacement. If we suppress emotional expression, then a trigger in the form of a person can receive a backlog of emotion that is not attributed to them, yet was not expressed at the appropriate time.

Triggers can be healers if their timing coincides with a readiness to let go of old, stagnant emotion. A readiness to clear one's emotional vehicle of blocks, along with a series of triggers that facilitate that, can lead to a state where the emotional vehicle is cleansed to the point that triggers no longer provoke the outbursts of emotional backlog. If the suppression of emotion no longer happens, then the emotional vehicle can be healed from a backlog of old, unexpressed emotion. The trigger can purge the vehicle by 'touching' the emotion and attracting it to the surface. If this happens with a sense of acceptance, then healing can occur. In a cleansed emotional vehicle where there is no suppression, everything is a trigger, and emotion is expressed freely and easily. Emotional expressions continually pour forth unrestricted by suppression.

Expression and repression

The nature of emotion is expression. This expression can be restrained by fear. A fearful situation can override the expression of an emotion and therefore suppress it. When we are frightened, we tense up, and physical and emotional flows are restricted. This is a freezing within the emotions brought about by the emotion of fear.

Emotion can also be suppressed by the application of a moral code. If we decide mentally what is and what is not allowed according to an arbitrary code, then the mind essentially rules the emotions. Whilst the emotion of fear may constrain emotional expression in a way that protects the organism, the application of moral code does not. The head simply cannot know what is best for the emotions until it has surrendered control over them. Since the application of a moral code is a mental attempt to control all the vehicles, it leads to an unhealthy state in which the mind rules all the vehicles without knowing what is healthy for them.

The moral code is the guidebook for the mind when it attempts to grasp control of the vehicles. In the case of emotional expression, the imposition of a moral code causes tension. This effort to conform to the code is strewn with stress and the frustration of failure. No moral code can be adhered to successfully. The very effort to follow a moral code causes failure. There is a constant falling short of behaving, feeling, doing and being as the code suggests. The effort to comply results in constant failure and finally a giving-up. The code crumbles of its own accord and is abandoned by the one who once gave their lives to its guidance. The guidance then comes from *what is easy.*

Our nature is that of ease. Any difficulty or tension that arises is a denial of that ease. It is even easy to allow this denial. Without a code guiding us, a natural draw towards what is easy moves us. Since isness is what it is without effort, ease is what we are.

If a river encounters an obstruction to its progress, it flows around it without fuss. It moves into any space given to it. It moves with ease. A fire is at ease when it dies. Difficulties are of the realm of human invention. They are born of the ability to deny. If there is an effort to channel emotions to align their expression with a moral code, then there is a denial of the ease with which emotions express themselves *by themselves*. This is a difficulty that takes the form of repression. Any emotion that is restrained from expressing itself by being channelled into a morally 'right' mode of expression stagnates and gathers tension. When the tension of an emotional flow becomes greater than the attempt to keep it repressed, it pours out. This outpouring is uncontrollable. When it happens, it is so obviously out of control that it can remind one that all of the previous 'controlling' of emotion was also like the outpouring – utterly uncontrollable.

This outpouring of repressed emotion happens whenever the moral code that is repressing it dissolves. The boundaries that were erected in the attempt to retain emotion fall away, and the emotion moves out. This is inevitable. No emotion can ever be stopped from expressing itself. Restraint of emotion in accordance with a moral code merely gives the appearance that the emotion's movement is postponed. Restraint of emotional expression serves to 'slow down' the movement of emotion and creates a backlog of it. Where there are attempts to stop emotional expression, the emotion seeps from a festering reservoir where it is being held, and becomes one's lifestyle.

In the case of the one who never allows sadness to express itself, they end up with a sad life that rarely *feels* sad. Even though deep expression of the emotion is absent, one's lifestyle mimics it in everything but direct expression. A 'controlled' emotion taints the lifestyle of the one who is attempting to control it. The richness of experience is thereby severely compromised in an attempt for 'safety'. To let all emotion flow without conditions and without overwhelming fear is to open up to the experience of the vibrant richness of the universe.

The futility of 'repressing' emotional expression is that emotion is in full expression whether or not there is an attempt to stop it. There is, therefore, a failure with every effort to stop an expression of emotion. This effort can cause a backlog of emotion that is limited to unconscious expression in the physical body. Aches, pains and illness are examples of this. With the falling apart of the moral code, there is no longer a 'right' way to express emotion. All the emotion that is unconsciously expressing itself in the physical body can move out beyond it. It is like the lid being taken off a pressure cooker. The pressure cooker builds and builds in tension with the moral code acting as the lid. The lid keeps the emotion internalized. When the moral code disappears, the lid comes off and the resulting movement of emotional expression is magnified, unpredictable and uncontrollable. In the case of anger this 'blowing of the lid' can take the form of screaming. With sadness, the form can be crying. A flow of emotional expression, unadulterated by a moral code, can clear a backlog built up by repression and opens up infinite options for that emotion's expression.

Any attempt to be free of an emotion before it has expressed itself in its own way, simply fuels the effort to keep it repressed. The deeper the repressive effort, the more unpredictable and violent the effects when the lid flies off the pressure cooker. If, when the lid comes off, there is no effort to put it back on, then the uncontrollable nature of emotion can be recognized. The attempt to regenerate the moral code is an effort to put the lid back on. If the moral code is accepted as dead without any attempt to revive it, then there is no attempt to fit into a 'right' way. When a moral is disallowing an emotional expression, the eventual direct expression of the emotion is a sign that the moral has died. The expression is not a means by which to kill a moral, but it is a simultaneous happening alongside the death of the once repressive moral. With the death of the moral code, and in the absence of strong fear, emotion can express itself without restraint, flowing anywhere and anyhow. When this happens, the steam from the pressure cooker can come out gently and continually, without the tensions of outbursts caused by a 'closed lid'.

Displacement and direct expression

Emotions seek expressions in appropriate forms. To facilitate emotional expression without restraint is to let them play themselves out. When an emotion arises, we can allow it to express itself in any form it chooses. With no restraints, the form will naturally be the one of greatest ease. Fluid expression of emotion is direct and easy.

This direct expression of emotion pre-empts suppression and clears potential backlogging of emotion. Any emotion naturally seeks expression with the person or thing that it associates with its uprising. If another deals with us in an angry way, this can touch anger in ourselves that will then seek expression back toward that person. This direct expression is natural and healthy. The alternative is suppression, which is commonly followed by displacement. In displacement, someone else receives the emotional expression even though they were unconnected with the event that accompanied the uprising of that feeling.

An emotion attaches itself to the person who was present when the emotion came into manifestation. The emotion is inherently connected to that person, and seeks reconnection with them through expression to them.

When we allow this to play itself out, we are free from emotional suppression and denial. We are also free from displacement. When we continually displace emotional expression, we are denying the emotions the chance to express themselves towards the person connected to the emotion in the first place.

An example of displacement is an event where someone hits you and anger rises up. Through either fear or moral control there is no immediate expression of that anger towards the one who hit you, so it is suppressed and channelled, and lies festering underneath the surface. Then, later on, an innocent person receives an exaggerated form of the anger. You scream at your partner who is always giving to you, for instance. If that anger had been displayed towards whoever hit you, it would not have been displaced. The results of displacement are a fragmentation of intimacy with whoever receives your anger later on.

If we freely and easily express emotion with the person who accompanied its uprising, then it feels appropriate and fresh. It is akin to a round peg fitting into a round hole on a children's peg-board. The emotion simply fits a mode of expression. To let the emotion fit into any expression that it chooses without moral intervention is to let *ease* take precedence. Particularly extreme emotional expression involving violent abuse is seldom the way of greatest ease, and is usually the result of a lengthy bout of suppression followed by an unpredictable outburst of displacement. A cleared emotion that is working effectively and efficiently will readily express itself as it arises.

Transparent emotional expression is a wonderful sharing. It is the open heart's response to emotion. It is a reflection of intimacy with another human. When we are honest and open with our emotions, we no longer hide from them. Personal grudges are the result of suppressed anger. To hold anger back when it is appropriately seeking expression with another human being is to build up resentment towards them. To be directly and openly angry with them is to be honest and to retain intimacy with them, regardless of their response. It also clears the physical body of the tension that results from suppression. Such tension can make the body ill, and one side effect of direct emotional expression is the clearance of long-standing physical blocks that arose through suppression.

To let emotion flow without restriction is to let the heart be flooded with openness. When there is clarity within the heart of perpetual newness and adventure, any emotion can express itself in any way, without fear for the consequences. The emotions are recognized to be part of who we are, yet not totally who we are. We can therefore relax our controlling influence on the emotional vehicle and let it drive itself. Interference can create physical illness, fragmented relationships, and a sense of isolation or desperation. We do not need to interfere. An open heart is one that lets all come and go without attempting to control the quantity and timing of it. Nor does it attempt to filter undesirable elements out. An open heart can lead one to recognition of one's essential nature as isness.

A closed heart denies this. It protects one's 'self' in a stance of exaggerated self-importance. This stance stands against anything that might strip the protection away and leave the heart naked and vulnerable. The irony of a closed heart is that the protection that it builds up is there to protect against the loss of that protection. A heart can only close in an attempt to break away from isness. It is an attempt to 'better' isness. The frustration of a closed heart is that no matter how much protection is built up, the heart still remains, at its core, open and vulnerable. The protection simply forms a surface layer that manifests as over-valued ego. We all have vulnerable, open hearts. A closed heart is simply one in denial of its inherent openness.

Children and emotions

Young children express the suppressed emotion of their parents. The parent will often attempt to stop the young child from expressing that emotion because it stimulates a similar uprising in them. They know that if it were let loose in themselves, it would be magnified and uncontrollable in its manifestation. Therefore, the common parental strategy is to force or encourage suppression in the child also. Whatever the parent tries to suppress in the child will grow and form the child's character traits. Children grow in the direction of that from which they are being restrained. This is commonly seen in teenage years where all the elements that the parents tried to suppress in the child bubble up into expression. This is seen as 'rebellion' by the parents. It is the child breaking out of the parents' influence and at last, with some relief, letting out all those aspects that the parents worked long and hard to suppress.

Inventing causes

The need to understand the 'causes' of emotions is a struggle with isness. Emotions rise uncaused. They can be triggered but they have no cause. The effort to extract a meaning from an emotion can lead one into confusion. To clear the confusion, a reason must be invented. Reasoning gives a feeling of safety. The safety that is sought is the assurance that the emotion will not last forever and will end at some time.

Emotions come and go regardless of our interference. The effort to understand emotional 'causes' is an attempt to see the matter clearly in the mind. The invention of all kinds of 'causes' serves to either 'protect' against the recurrence of that emotion or to 'rekindle' that emotion by triggering it once again. The logic goes: 'If the cause is known, I can either avoid the emotion or stimulate it again.' By avoiding the 'cause', it is hoped that the emotion itself will be avoided. And by going towards the 'cause', it is hoped that the emotion will be felt again. Yet, inevitably, the emotion pops up again with or without the 'cause' being present. Emotions come and go independent of circumstance. The circumstance may trigger the emotional rising but it is not the cause. There simply is no cause. The belief in cause-and-effect is an extrapolation of perceptions from our day-to-day actions into the invisible realm of mind, emotion, and being. The perception that we are the cause of effects around us leads to the view that everything must have a cause. Yet, if we accept that we are equally as much an effect as a cause, then the whole issue of cause-and-effect is without meaning.

Sadness

According to the moral code sadness is often labelled as 'bad' and happiness as 'good'. Following such a code, the 'ups' and 'downs' that are seen in life are judged to be 'good' when you are 'up' and 'bad' when you are 'down'. Such judgement, if taken to heart, excludes enjoyment. Sadness can be equally as enjoyable as happiness, but if we believe that enjoyment only comes with happiness, and if this is all that can be enjoyed, then sadness will seem to steal the joy from life. However, sadness and joy *can* exist alongside each other. If there is no urgent need to better life as it is, then there is no block to the enjoyment of sadness. Times of sadness are useful and functional. They offer time for rest, healing and reflection. Yet, the disdain with which sadness is treated by most moral codes blocks this healthy, natural process. The push to end sadness is a non-acceptance of it. Anything that happens in life that is not accepted is pushed deeper through repression and can severely taint one's lifestyle. To avoid sadness is to disrespect its function and postpone the dispersion of it. Any suppression of our emotional expression serves to push that emotion deeper down into the subconscious mind and physical body.

To be sad without attachment and without aversion is to let it pass swiftly and healthily. To hold onto or to ignore sadness is to become stuck in a sad lifestyle. Someone who is attached to sadness seeks identity through it, and often enjoys the attention and helplessness that comes with it. They are seeking for others to care for them and a useful strategy is to hold on to sadness as a continual character trait, thereby attracting the sympathy and concern of others. The one who has an aversion to sadness lives in the 'let's-pretend' realm of happiness. They pretend that they are happy, and often will blame others if the happiness disappears. They claim to be happy and that sadness is 'wrong' or 'bad'. They deny sadness, even though their lifestyle is tainted with sadness. With the attempted repression of sadness, psychological illnesses such as depression can develop.

Sadness cannot be 'cured'. The ease of sadness is to be sad with an open heart that lets it in as far as it goes, with no restriction. This destroys the attachment to the sadness. With no attachment or involvement, the sadness weaves its way into expression and is gone. All sadness comes and goes. With no attempt to repress it, it goes more quickly. With an attempt to repress it, it lingers and is postponed. Eventually a repressed sadness will go too, upon physical death if not before. If there is an insistent effort to become free of sadness because it 'is bad', 'is wrong', 'is not allowed', 'should be over by now', or 'can't be this way because of external circumstances', then this sadness will be given attention in the form of avoidance. Such an involvement in a natural process serves to make sadness a centre-point of one's life. Instead of letting it run its course, the effort to end it *prolongs* it, and pushes it deeper into the subconscious.

With a constant grasping at more 'ups' and less 'downs', life turns into a series of 'downs' with brief respites in the 'ups'. The 'ups' cannot even be enjoyed for fear of another 'down'. If full enjoyment of the 'ups' *and* 'downs' is experienced, then the fear of, or even the preference for, one or the other fades away. This is not to discount a natural response of the heart to come out of a depression that was caused by stuck sadness. If a heart-felt movement away from depression into elation is experienced, then to follow this is healthy. The difference between following one's heart and following a moral code is that the heart genuinely knows what is best for the vehicles. To follow the heart takes no effort. To follow morals takes much effort.

To hear the heart's signal in amongst the noise of the mind, body and feelings is to find a steady stillness where focus can single out that most quiet of voices. To hear the heart is a rich experience. It grounds one in the security of giving control up to the core of our being. When we move from the core, we can be fulfilled all the way through. If we only move from the periphery, then the vehicles may find temporary fulfilment but the depth of fulfilment is not as vast as when we experience it from a heart connection.

An open heart can respond to sadness in a way that is appropriate to our being as a whole. Either it directs the vehicles to experience the sadness fully, without getting stuck in it, or it directs the move away from it temporarily by using distraction. The sincerity of such a motivation lies in the fact that sadness has not been permanently avoided. It is eventually allowed to run its course by being experienced fully. The heart does not wish for the vehicles to get stuck in sadness once the sadness has run its course, and therefore directs the move out of it at the appropriate time.

Fear and malice

Malice is a form of aggressive denial. The source of malice is fear. When there is an urgent fear of vulnerability, then the will to protect one's 'self' becomes extreme. To fear what one is, is to fight it with aggressive denial. So, any malice is actually malice toward one's own 'self' as an attempt to break it and somehow become different.

Inappropriate submission can be used in a similar way. Submission can be the hope that someone else will break one's 'self', thereby 'releasing' one back into the realm of no-separation. To be content with isness is to rest. In contentment with what is, aggression and submission are accepted, and neither is denied expression. Fear is also accepted. And, perhaps most remarkably, the final disappearance of fear is also accepted.

Fear's function is to protect the vehicles and ensure their survival. However, when we utilize that instinct at a deeper level, we disengage from life and the flow of spirit into form becomes obstructed by tightness. When one uses fear in an attempt to protect one's 'self' from being absorbed in isness, then one feels isolated from isness. To let this fear go is very frightening, as the perceived security of isolation must be surrendered.

The greatest fear is the total destruction of fear. With no fear, there is no protection for one's 'self'. Fear still functions to protect the mental, emotional and physical vehicles, but there is 'nobody' who does the fearing. This is the total destruction of fear as a 'done' action. To release such a deep response is to accept one's essential unity and dance without fear to the song of the heart.

8 *Relationships*

To be intimate is to be transparent. To honour love with another human is to be who you are with them. To authentically be who you are is to let expressions move unconstrained. If you try to hide your nature from another, you can only do so by deceit. To be open and transparent with another no matter how this manifests is to be honest with them. Here lies intimacy.

Honesty and deception

Honesty in a loving relationship can destroy one's chances of 'getting' something. To be honest with another is to sacrifice deception. Deception is commonly used as a strategy to 'gain' something for one's self. Honesty leaves one openly transparent with no advantage. When you are honest, you are easy to read. Deception can be employed to mask motives. If deception is employed, the heart closes and keeps a secret. This hiding can be used to cloud another's vision of us. The idea behind this deception is that one can 'get' something more easily without the other noticing. This can be done before it is 'too late'. This urgency is propelled by the fear that if it is not 'got as soon as possible', it may never be got.

Deception can happen consciously or unconsciously. However, the strategy is the same – close the heart so that someone is shut out, go to 'get' something, then hope that the other does not find out or then be honest once the desired thing has been 'obtained'. The effort to 'get' something from a relationship, or to make life 'better' through interacting in one, is a constant upheaval. The strategies that are employed in order to help the effort to succeed can include secrecy, deception, dishonesty and avoidance.

For the one whose struggle has ended, there is no need to 'get' anything out of relationships. Honesty is allowed into the expression of mind, body and emotions. Sexual pulls can be explored without secrecy. With no intention or motivation to 'gain' something from a relationship, all relationships can flow spontaneously and with ease. Nothing needs to be hidden. We can be open-hearted without the protection of ego projection. Projection of the ego is a protective measure that suggests that 'you and I are separate'. An open heart that is falling into absorption no longer needs to obsessively hold onto this protection. Absorption is simply not possible without vulnerability. To protect one's 'self' takes effort. With vulnerability can come the revelation that we have always been vulnerable and that all the hard efforts to 'protect' our 'selves' only *appeared* to work.

Getting and desiring

To desire something is natural. Our physical body, mind and emotions are often drawn to something out of desire. Suppressing desire strengthens it and increases the possibility that the desire will return. Pushing to fulfil a desire also strengthens the possibility that it will return because the first time around was unsatisfying.

A desire in and of itself can be satisfying to the point that the fulfilment or non-fulfilment of it are equally irrelevant. To savour a desire fully without suppression or urgency is to delight in the experience of it. Such a delight of experience is so satisfying and is a hallmark of a non-grasping, open heart. If, however, there is suppression (trying for non-fulfilment) or urgency (trying for fulfilment), this is our conditioning and need not be changed. If we have wants then fulfilment is a natural goal. If we have aversions, non-fulfilment is a natural goal. To have wants or aversions and to try to get rid of them is a non-acceptance and a denial of isness.

Wants and aversions are fear-driven. There is an anxiety that either 'something should be got now because there may be no other chance' (urgent wanting) or 'something should not be got because getting it may be damaging' (protective, suppressive aversion). In both cases, fear is a factor. Urgency to 'get' is the fear of never being able to have what it is that is tried for. Suppressing in order to 'not get' is the fear that something may be harmful and should be avoided. Conditioning and the moral code invite us to invest in ownership and then protect what we 'own'. If and when fear falls away, we are 'freed' from ownership and protection.

To be in the midst of a collapsing moral code is to witness isness with increasing clarity. With no mental reference-point to tell us how to live, we can recognize the equality of isness and see that we are no more or less important then anyone or anything else. Importance is a human invention. It is based on the moral judgement values of 'better' and 'worse'. Judgement does not cause importance, but holding onto judgement does. When a human judges himself or herself to be 'better' than someone or something else, then this a functional comparison. However, if the judgement is grasped and held onto by a greedy heart then exaggerated self-importance arises. Such self-importance is not 'wrong' or 'bad', it is simply a denial of isness. That nothing is more or less important than anything else is denied in order to 'get' something. If the denial were not there, then an open heart would recognize that *there is nothing to 'get'*. An open heart continues to respond to the desires of the expressive vehicles but it has no need to 'get' for itself. We can then rest in our absorption in isness without needing to deny it in order to create a purpose that is then used to justify 'getting'. Struggle is in trying to 'better' isness by 'getting more'. Contentment is in accepting isness.

Possessiveness and jealousy

Possessiveness is sublime and often goes unnoticed until it is threatened. When the effort to own someone comes under pressure, there are only two options of change – to tighten the shackles of grasping, or to let go. The letting go is painful, as is all loss. Yet, the pain does not last forever and even if it did, it is only when we let go of another that intimacy can deepen with them. When we simply accept that in our hearts we own nothing, including our 'selves', then we can relax from the struggle of perpetually holding on. We can let all be as it is without a will to change it or better it. This is such a delightful rest!

When we let someone go, only then can we dissolve into him or her. Allowing them to be who they are, even if *they* do not know who they are, and even if this is painful, is the key to merging into another. Love holds no boundaries. However, the fear of losing control holds up many boundaries. These boundaries are set up in an attempt to stop the overwhelming beauty and magnificence of the universe from pervading our hearts. The fear is 'what will happen to me if I let everything in?' The unbounded realms of love allow us to be who we are with open hearts. There is no longer a filter in the heart that determines what is preferable to let in. All preferences of the heart vanish as it flowers and opens. All that is left then is response.

Of course, we all know, whether consciously or not, that dropping the significance of boundaries leads to the ruination of exaggerated self-importance. This sense of self-importance was derived from our coping mechanisms. It was derived from our attempted separation from isness by a closing of the heart. It was derived from our attempts to go beyond isness and become something that cannot be hurt. Yet hurt is an integral part of life. Without it, the emotional responses to pleasure would not exist. We rely on pain as a vehicular guide, and also as a contrast. Without pain, we simply would not know pleasure.

The pain that one feels from witnessing another's expression of 'freedom' is one of 'letting go of holding on'. When we hold onto another and attempt to keep them, and they then move beyond our attempt to control their closeness to us, then we recognize their autonomy. Seeing their sheer uncontrollability can seem daunting and painful yet it is merely an honest awareness of how it has always been and how it always will be.

Jealousy is the recognition that we never owned someone. Through habit and patterns built up by routine, we can become convinced that we have 'ownership' of someone. When we recognize that we do not own them, this perception gets shattered within the emotion of jealousy. Jealousy can be wonderfully healing. It can be a tempestuous awakening of suppressed feelings. If allowed expression, jealousy can expose fundamental dishonesty in the one experiencing jealousy, and sometimes also in the one triggering it.

Receptivity

To experience balance in relationships, the open heart must manifest in the body and feelings as *a capacity to receive*. To receive is to be open to all input.

When this happens in the body, we let sensory awareness become expansive to the point that the input can become totally overwhelming. We then become flooded with orgasmic energy that is discharged in sexual climax, deep breathing and vocalizations. The depth of surrender to this energy denotes the depth of sexual satisfaction that is experienced. In sexuality it is the depth of experience, not the breadth of experimentation, that is ultimately satisfying.

To openly receive in our feeling is to allow the feelings of another to touch our feelings. With such a vulnerable sharing of emotion, we 'become' another in as much as we are able to experience how they are feeling by feeling it ourselves. This is empathy, and bonds couples in a similar way that satisfying sexual union does. When the level of receptivity is high enough in both members of a couple, a vulnerable sharing exists where bodies and feelings can deeply merge. While we need to spend time in bodily and emotional independence to balance this merging, it is the capacity to merge in vulnerability that unites couples in a relationship.

To receive is to let down defences and boundaries. If we are guarded against input from our partner, because of past trauma or suspicion, we cannot fully let them in and merging cannot occur. Under these circumstances, the unconscious strategy of 'give-to-get' may be implemented. Since there is a lack of satisfaction due to a reduced capacity to receive, and since the move toward satisfaction is healthy, a bias towards giving can emerge. The hope is that if enough is given, then finally satisfaction will be experienced in receiving. However, if we have a diminished receptivity, no matter how much attention, energy or acts of love are returned to us, we cannot receive them and they appear unsatisfying. This can be very frustrating. We give to others continually (albeit for selfish reasons) yet it seems as though what we get back does not balance with the giving. If this frustration is then vented at the other in a relationship, then we use them as a scapegoat to deny our own lack of receptivity.

The blocks to receptivity are often rooted in fear. It can be frightening to receive since we are vulnerable in the act of it. Yet it is only when we get in touch with this fear, and feel it fully, that we can cease *living* in fear. When we can fully feel fear, and can befriend it, it no longer disturbs us and we no longer live by it as a main motivator. We can feel fear *and* let something or someone in. However, if fear is there and we dissociate from that feeling, then it forms a defence against input. If we are not strong enough, or ready enough, to feel scared then the fear becomes frozen and forms a block to receptivity. Reconnecting with this fear can release those blocks.

When our receptivity opens up, we illuminate the capacity to merge sensually, sexually, erotically, physically, or emotionally into another. This amazing vulnerability allows a deep bond to develop between couples, and is the essence of all relationship bonding.

Melting into the one heart

We *are love*. Love is who we are, what we are made of, what we are inside of, and what we contain. To honour our essential nature as one of love is to give up making efforts to relate. When love is recognized to be *in* the heart, *of* the heart and *as* the heart, then we can relax our hold in relationships. Without this spontaneous, uncaused and continual recognition, one seeks for a stirring of it through relationships. These relationships are with other humans, places, rituals, religions, substances or objects.

Once we see that the love we experience for another is not dependent on them, we can get over an obsession with objects of love. It is then that the clarity of our nature *as* love can open up. To be in love with another is to share the recognition that we *are* love. The other does not cause the love. The love is simply our nature waiting to be discovered through vulnerability. To be vulnerable and open with another is to honour the intimacy that all parts within the whole share.

A loved one can encourage us to bare our heart. With a bare heart, there are no barriers to intimacy, and the essence of the heart as love can be recognized clearly once again. Typically, this is a glimpse of unbounded love and the one struck by it often associates the object as the cause. This glimpse feels so wonderful and there may be a tendency to want to keep feeling that way. The object can then be clung onto in desperation, with a belief that the object somehow 'caused' the love. This can happen even after the feeling has subsided. Such is the pattern of 'falling in and out of love'. This is a pattern of a heart opening and closing: opening to be naked and humble then closing through the fear that now there is no protection.

There is no protection of the heart in love. To let our boundaries dissolve, and to be naked-hearted without protection is to reconnect with the love that we are. When this happens in the 'safety' of another's company, we can associate an external factor as being the root of intimacy. A partner, sexual interaction, emotional sharing or anything that facilitates the release from a holding into an open-hearted vulnerability is not the root of intimacy. It is the trigger that can fuel our recognition that the experience of love, sharing and intimacy are always part of 'I'.

To be vulnerable with another is to melt into them. In this meeting, the force of reconnection pours through. Importance of self over others cannot survive here. To retain a sense of importance over others, one must push away from intimacy and continue to protect one's 'separate self'. To let the barriers down would be to recognize the shocking denial of attempting to be separate. To melt into another is to relinquish 'control' and to be in equality. When (and if) this happens, it is so easy, whereas it is very difficult to maintain an effort to be in 'control' and to protect the heart.

To honour our nature as love is to effortlessly have no need to protect our heart. All is love and is recognized as such. There are no barriers to intimacy where such an honour resides. Intimacy *is* vulnerability. It is the acceptance that since we are all one love, then anything that can be 'taken' from the whole actually remains in the whole. There is then no motive to protect an individual heart. When we melt into love without protection, we can recognize that there is only one heart. All individuality of heart is fear-based protection. To melt into the one heart is to give up all sense of self-importance and all effort to relate. When we honour the unity of the love that we are, we can recognize it clearly everywhere. Attachment to certain objects, including people, is not necessary as the heart is always filled with the love that was once sought for in externals. With an open, vulnerable and effortless heart, our nature *as love* radiates into all other aspects of love.

Who do they think you are?

There can come a time when we stop running away from what life is perpetually offering us. We can stay still amongst the splendour of existence without turning to an escape route or a solution. We can dissolve into that which is too vast for words. We can stand humble and in awe while the gigantic beauty of isness swallows us whole. To be amongst such a glorious happening is to spontaneously honour one's nature. Honour is the essence of following through with who we are. When we are absorbed in isness and honouring all that life is, then we can see that we are being who we are. This being comes without effort and cannot be contained by another's perceptions.

Everyone paints pictures in their mind of who everyone else is. This is functional. It is imagination. Yet, believing these pictures to be an accurate reference to who another is distances us from clearly seeing who they are. We can form so many ideas about another, put labels on them, think we know them, think we know what they are doing, and generally derive a sense of confidence from believing that we have others totally figured out. However, as soon as someone breaks our image of who we imagined him or her to be, then we meet with doubt. The belief wavers and finally falls flat on its face. When we open-heartedly acknowledge that we do not know whom someone else is, then we can *be* him or her.

Knowing someone is dependent on having a relationship to them. Being them is to become them, and see through their eyes, from their perspective. Being someone is to behold him or her without an imaginative belief about who they are. Imagination is not dangerous. It simply does not reflect accurately upon the material world. If we awake from a dream in which we are being chased, and start to run around the room, others can see the inaccuracy. Likewise, if we fantasize about what another is doing and act from that fantasy only to find out they are doing something different, then we discover inaccuracy. Imagination is wonderfully creative but it is not reliable as a reference point to happenings of the material world.

When another decides that they have us pinned down in a certain category, and we do not correspond to the behaviour that they expect, they may try to dissuade us from shattering their image of us by pressuring us to conform. So it is in families. Human beings who have been together in a period of growth can often believe that they know each other. If one suddenly begins to honour their nature, the others may be confused and frustrated. They may attempt to encourage the other to conform to their beliefs of who they think them to be, or who they want them to be. If the other continues to honour their nature, resentment may ensue. To honour your nature is to veer away from the role that others hold you to, and this may be responded to with contempt.

Such is the saga of breaking family patterns. The family is held together by tightly-knit patterns. When someone breaks those patterns, it threatens the whole meaning of what it is to be in a family. When this threat is accepted, then we can allow the meaning of family to open up to a much wider context than simply blood-relatives. It can include friends, animals, places, and ultimately everything that has ever been experienced.

To honour your nature amongst pressure from family members to conform is by far the greatest test of whether the honour is resilient or not. To open-heartedly recognize who you are in the face of commotion, accusation, resentment, hostility, aggression, pain, fear, and doubt is to see that being who you are is not only extremely easy, but that it happens even under extreme pressure.

Accepting the other

Part of acceptance is forgiveness without obligation. When we accept someone, we forgive all their past actions and the obligation to bear responsibility for these actions ceases. There may exist the temptation to carry the responsibility for someone else's conditioned actions. It can appear tempting in as much as the victim role can then be taken up. Someone taking up the victim role has a reliable method for attention-seeking whereby they grieve the past actions of another.

Hostile acts are often a cry for help. If someone has treated us in a hostile way, we are not obliged to respond to him or her by carrying his or her actions with us. We can let the past be the past without regret, and without urgently wanting to change it. When we are in forgiveness, we can see someone for who they are and we cease to blame them for being that. Everyone is conditioned. Everyone acts according to his or her conditioning.

Everyone has had agony and trauma in their lives. No one has ever lived without it. Where trauma is concerned, the major distinction between humans is in their capacity to accept. Non-acceptance is to take on the role of a victim. Acceptance is forgiveness without obligation. When we forgive another for their actions, we simply accept them for who they are. We accept that their mind, body and emotions are all conditioned and that they are not responsible for that conditioning and *nor are we*. We no longer feel obliged to respond to their cry for help by carrying the anxiety of their actions.

If we believe strongly that we have had an unfortunate past, then we ignore our fortune. Likewise, if we convince ourselves that our past has been fortunate then we ignore our misfortune. When we are dealt a hand of cards in life, we can only play them to our full potential when we accept our cards as they are.

The victim

The victim role is successfully played out by those who wish that they could escape from isness but know that they do not have the mechanisms to do so. The victim cannot admit to himself or herself that there is no escape from isness, yet they know that they have no means with which to attempt it. As a 'solution', the victim dons the role of 'the one who has been hard done by'. The victim calls on others to reinforce this role by repeatedly blaming those around them for the circumstances of their life. The victim cries out for support from others in an obsessive and abusive manner. They wish that others would deliver them from the hell of isness. Yet, there is no deliverance from isness. The only deliverance can be from the hell of it, and this can only come through surrender. Since no one can give us surrender, and no one can let go for us, the victim never manages to release his or her grip on isness. They play the controlling game that tries to keep everything 'above water' whilst at the same time knowing that they will not succeed. To let go of the victim role is to die into the extremities of honesty. It is to release the fear of the heart in a flourishing of forgiveness. Once forgiveness pours unrestrained through the heart, there no longer needs to be a reason for forgiving another, and therefore no grudge held against them.

Love heals us naturally when we give up the victim role. When we lay to rest that old record that says 'I had it real tough, I had it bad,' then we can awake to the glory of existence. When we throw away the role of victim and become stronger for it, then the flow of abuse from one human to another is easily stunted. We can take an emotional, physical or psychic stance against any such abuse. We do not need to tolerate abuse, and can fight those who are wielding it. If, when it happens, we do not fight those who abuse us, then we will abuse others. This is how the cycle of abuse perpetuates itself. To stunt the flow of abuse is to wholeheartedly lay down denial and resentment, and fight those who abuse us with forgiveness and faith in our hearts.

The emotions seek resolution in abusive relationships. The physical body responds, and can grow in strength and posture. When we let out the anger we feel about those who have abused us, without grudge or anxiety, then we can clearly let go of those scars and wounds that were once used to gain affection and attention. Without these wounds, the world opens up into infinite options as we find the victim role vanishes, and who we are shines forth.

We cannot stop abuse in the world. We can only experience the purging of the abuse that we have carefully carried within ourselves for so long. When this purging happens, we lose our wounds, and with it the victim role. Then the need to perpetuate abuse in the world vanishes.

Conflict

Conflict performs a useful function in relationships. It serves to bring to light a difference between the desires of two humans. Many moral codes outlaw conflict, labelling it as 'wrong'. However, the suppression of conflict produces poison in relationships. To honestly and unashamedly show another that there is a conflict of differences between desires is healthy. If it is taken as a serious fight then we may take responsibility for it and morally scold ourselves for 'wrongful' behaviour. However, if we are open to conflict arising in us without our control, then we can let it take its course without our interference, suppression or encouragement.

Conflict is healthy when it marks the difference between desires, and plays them off against each other. All desires move towards fulfilment. If we let them do this without concern for the outcome, then conflict is not a problem. We can have a relaxed battle for fulfilment and have no preference for 'winning' or 'losing' our fulfilment of desire. Desires are a continual flow. No one ever got rid of desire altogether. So, if one desire is unfulfilled, another will soon come along to become the focus of a move toward fulfilment. To recognize this is to lose the anxiety associated with fulfilment or non-fulfilment of desires.

Addiction

Addiction is an obsessive relationship with something. The 'take it or leave it' attitude that prevails in open relationships is narrowed and closed to a 'must have it' in addiction. The addictive relationship obsessively returns someone to an object, be it a drug, place, other human, food, sex, activity, experience or feeling.

In addiction, there is a limited capacity for unpredictability. The relationship of the addict with the object of their addiction is a monotonous, predictable one. It is so devoid of spontaneity that the addict, at the same time as obsessively interacting with their object, is bored and frustrated both with the obsession and the object of addiction itself. The addict manages to maintain their holding-on behaviour through denial. Denial is the only strategy that the addict can fall back on in order to continue their addictive relationship. Honesty could completely wreck an addict's continuation with their addiction.

Addiction is born out of an experienced lack of wholeness. The addict therefore uses the object of their addiction in an attempt to feel whole. A typical scenario is when one's life goes through a 'bad' patch. Here, again, the moral code works its influence. The 'bad' patch 'should not be there' according to a moral code that says "get more goodness in life and less bad!" An object of addiction can be used in an attempt to make life better, when all that is needed is an openness to a temporary discomfort. Someone who tries to give up their addiction by forcing away the object of addiction ends up in a new kind of denial – one of denying an existing addictive relationship. If an addiction is to be transcended, then the relationship to the object of that addiction must return to an easy 'take it or leave it' relationship.

An open heart does not obsessively guard against addictive impulses. It does not hold onto anything in an effort to better isness. It accepts isness. An addict cannot cure the addiction through a different style of denial. The addiction can only die when the addict's heart opens beyond a 'need to get more', and beyond an urgent effort to better isness. They must feel strong and whole in themselves *as they are* before the object of addiction can be released in openness. Addiction slips away as our hearts grow and as we accept isness without any need to change it. Addictive behaviour requires a lack of experienced unity to sustain it. With a heart that has given up the attempt to control, we are graced with the refinement of addictive urges. It is then that the objects of addiction can return into open relationships.

Addiction at its most gross level is an exclusive obsession with one particular type of experience. At its most refined level it is a released passion for experience in *any form*. The depth or shallowness of anything we experience depends primarily on our experience, not on the thing itself. Therefore, if we have a very deep experience of something, it is the experience that is deep, not the thing. Similarly, if we experience something as being shallow, it is a shallow experience, not a shallow thing.

Commonly, the addictive obsession is with a certain kind of pleasurable experience. Someone addicted at the gross level will repetitively return to the object to replay that experience. They are passionate for the object and its experience to the exclusion of passion for other experiences. A pleasure-seeking addict will tend to cower from painful experience. They can use denial in an attempt to convince themselves that 'only what they want exists'. Denying isness in such a way confines the richness of experience. Someone who is obsessed with one type of experience, and who uses denial in an effort to stay exclusively within that experience, tries to narrow down the infinite nature of experience to their one preferred experience. Inevitably, no matter how hard the addict tries, that one experience does not remain. Experiences come and go. When the experience that the addict is obsessed with goes, the addict withdraws from subsequent experience by heart-closing and dishonesty. It is only when their obsessively chosen experience returns that they can embrace it intimately. The rest of experience is shut off to. In this way, the addict not only reinforces their obsession with one particular type of experience, but the shock of being intimate with experiences that they did not choose seems too much to bear. In short, they 'shut off' from life in an attempt to protect the experience that they are obsessed with from being interrupted.

The refinement of addiction is a transformation of the manifestation of addictive behaviour. Addictive behaviour without obsession is an irrepressible passion for life and existence. To suppress addictive behaviour is to withdraw from this passion and live in a dull relationship to existence. The refinement of addiction, however, involves allowing addictive behaviour to continue whilst letting the obsession widen out. This widening out occurs when the person gradually recognizes their own inherent unity and no longer relies on the object of addiction to fill a lack of wholeness. A first step in such a widening can be the transition from harmful objects to benign ones. In the case of drug addiction, the person can progress through a series of substances, being addicted to each one, and giving each one up for a more benign one. Eventually, in such a process, the person learns the art of 'letting go'. They have still picked up a substitute drug, but in doing so, they have experienced their capacity to release and also minimized mental, emotional, physical, and social damage by switching to a more benign substance. It may be that the obsession is loosened so much that the addiction is not concentrated on substances any more. Then the addictive behaviour can be released from obsession and the person can relish experiences as a whole. When one has an equal passion for all experiences, then one is free from the shackles of obsession. One is then enriched in existence by the intimacy with every experience. The heart can remain open and there is no 'precious obsession' to try to protect. One can bathe in the continued recognition of essential wholeness.

Addiction manifests at the peak of refinement as an addiction to the experience of existence. It is an explorative curiosity that is wide open and is not obsessed with the collection of certain types of experiences. All is welcome to enter the heart. This is a wondrous dance of intimacy with the elements of isness. It is an exploration of infinite unity. This unity carries a familiar flavour. An open heart can recognize that we are this unity. This is who 'you' are, 'I' am, and everyone and everything is.

9 *Being Love*

To be in love is to see divinity. It is the sweet recognition of inherently being all that is. When we are that being, then the recognition vanishes. We are no longer in love with what is. We *are* love. And we are isness.

To be *in* love is a gentle embrace of being. Being in love is an embrace of our nature. Being in love holds the potential to lead us to honour our original state of being *of* love. To be *of* love is to dissolve in being. We have always been love and always will be. Being love is simply an honouring of our nature.

Only an open heart can be love. Only a heart that is merged with everything can be love. Our heart is, and always has been, merged with everything. Any attempt to separate our heart from isness is fuelled by learnt responses to fear and pain. The response is to close the heart and keep out all the undesirable elements of existence. Our ancestors and those around us give this undesirable judgement to us.

A closed heart forms a crystallized self around it. The motivations of this self are based on that which is being shut out. Shut out anything and that very resistance draws together to become the 'self'. Denial results from the reluctance to move toward what is resisted. A closed heart denies what it has become, and denies what motivates the self that has crystallized around it. The crystallized self around a closed heart acts as a buffer, keeping intimacy at a safe distance. Intimacy destroys the self and melts a closed heart.

Doing what you love

Naturally, we move towards doing what we love. Enjoying this is so easy. To honour the heart is to dissolve into it. If we give our life over to the directive of the heart, then we *are* our heart. There is no effort in this, only an acceptance of whatever happens as a result of honouring the heart. To follow the voice of the heart, without regard for the consequences, is to flourish in a bursting blossoming. Whatever your heart moves you to be, honour it, and even if all appears to break down, the contented rest of being who you are with honour will bring you the recognition that this existence is swimming with infinite passion. You awaken to the sheer beauty of all that is when you honour your heart.

Thinking, feeling, physical cravings, and desires all manifest as usual when we honour our heart. The difference is that we no longer listen to them or use them as an important strategy to prevent our 'self' from falling apart. We can honour them as functional for the survival of the vehicles, yet there is no longer an impulse to make them into something more than that by giving them more importance than our heart. When we follow our heart, we can rest. When we place ideas, thoughts, feelings, intuition, presumptions, expectations, hopes or fears before our heart, then we continue to struggle. To hear our heart is the easiest thing. When we give up making noise, all is heard clearly.

Giving up is amazingly refreshing. It is *not* a refusal or rejection of the world, rather an absence of effort. *Life lives itself.* Any effort we make to live life interferes with our enjoyment of this astonishingly natural process. Simplicity is letting life live itself. This is what is happening. Whether we fret or relax, control or surrender, invest or let go, push or rest, life lives itself. Everything continues to 'happen' regardless of our relationship to that happening. Our perception of happenings may differ according to our relationship to it but the happening itself is not dependent on anything.

Following the heart is the first condition for singing one's own song. We cannot rely on any authority to tell us who we are or how we should be it. If we look to others for authority, we can try to follow *their* hearts. What we end up following, though, is their heart's *response* to their mental, physical and emotional desires. If we look to our own heart for authority we can follow it, and recognize that 'our' heart and 'their' heart are the same heart. There is only one heart. The one heart responds in many ways to the many vehicles that express it.

The surrender to isness initially takes the form of following the heart. This matures into honouring our nature as a heart. The heart spontaneously recognizes the desires of the mind, emotions and physical body. All these vehicles can be seen by the heart and responded to accordingly. When an open heart has let struggle cease, it still responds to the desires of the vehicles, but it moves them toward the fulfilment of desires without an investment in the fulfilment. An open heart has a preference to move toward a vehicle's desired direction but has no preference as to whether or not that desire is fulfilled.

In a state of stillness, it becomes clear that nothing needs us to 'do it'. The sea rolls on, the clouds continue to form, thoughts come, our bodies keep on operating, emotions arise, desires crystallize, and experiences emerge. When we stop 'doing' these things, it is clear that we were never doing them in the first place. They were simply happening independent of our involvement.

We do not need to *do* who we are to *be* who we are. The doing can happen. We do not have to 'do' the happening of doing. It happens independent of control, like everything. We can relax in contentment as the grand adventure of isness plays itself out.

The unity of being love

With the recognition and honour of your essential nature as a whole being, your life will open and grow beyond imagination. Once you have seen again your inherent nature, then follow it in an honouring of that, you will experience the delicious opening-up of life. This will continue indefinitely. It is this growth that gives the feeling of being alive. The values of unity, love, security, responsibility, playfulness, courage, passion, health and joy will run steadily through your experience. This is the way of isness. This is the gift that is experienced when you align yourself with that which you are. When the struggle spontaneously dissolves, the heart can take over. The heart waits and waits, forever if need be, until that flowering happens and it can once again direct your life. For it is a life lived from the heart that heals the experience of separation between spirit and matter. When you live *as* love, *for* love, then the inherent unity that you already are will be appreciated in its entirety. May you be blessed with such a joyous life.